Acclaim for

AMITAV GHOSH'S

IN AN ANTIQUE LAND

"Delightful . . . This curious book [is] a mixture of history, travelogue, social anthropology and personal memoir. Ghosh skillfully draws our attention to parallels and contrasts to both the medieval and the modern stories." —*Washington Post Book World*

"Ghosh has found his own distinctive voice—polished and profound . . . wistful in its tone, assured in its achieved vision."
—*The Times Literary Supplement* (London)

"Remarkable . . . Ghosh uses his writing skill to create captivating vignettes, [and] offers a subtle glimpse into ordinary life in contemporary rural Egypt in a manner that at times rivals anything by the masters of social realism in modern Egyptian literature. The painstaking research and astonishing attention paid to minute details [are] admirable. [Ghosh is] an uncannily honest writer."
—Anton Shammas, *The New York Times Book Review*

"An inviting travel tale . . . *In an Antique Land* revolves around Egypt past, present and metaphorical, and relies on a large assemblage of characters to give [it] shape. Ghosh details the various stories in this book with energetic descriptions and his own research."
—*San Francisco Chronicle*

AMITAV GHOSH
IN AN ANTIQUE LAND

Amitav Ghosh was born in Calcutta in 1956 and studied in New Delhi, Oxford and Alexandria. He has traveled extensively throughout Europe, the Middle East and North Africa and has taught at New Delhi, the University of Virginia and Columbia University. He is the author of two widely acclaimed novels, *The Circle of Reason* and *The Shadow Lines*.

BOOKS BY AMITAV GHOSH

The Circle of Reason
The Shadow Lines
In an Antique Land

IN AN ANTIQUE LAND

IN AN ANTIQUE LAND

AMITAV GHOSH

VINTAGE DEPARTURES

Vintage Books

A Division of Random House, Inc.

New York

FIRST VINTAGE DEPARTURES EDITION, APRIL 1994

Library of Congress Cataloging-in-Publication Data
Ghosh, Amitav.
In an antique land/Amitav Ghosh.—1st Vintage Departures ed.
p. cm.
Originally published: New York: A. A. Knopf, 1993.
ISBN 0-679-72783-3
1. Ghosh, Amitav—Journeys—Egypt. 2. Ben Yijû, Abraham 12th cent.
3. Merchants, Jewish—Egypt—Biography. 4. Bomma, 12th cent.
5. Slaves—Egypt—Biography. I. Title.
DT56.2.G48 1994
916.204′.2—dc20 93-43555
CIP

Author photograph © Jerry Bauer

Manufactured in the United States of America
10 9 8 7 6 5 4 3

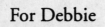
For Debbie

CONTENTS

Prologue   11

Laṭaîfa   21
Nashâwy   107
Mangalore   239
Going Back   289

Epilogue   343

Notes   355

PROLOGUE

THE SLAVE OF MS H.6 first stepped upon the stage of modern history in 1942. His was a brief debut, in the obscurest of theatres, and he was scarcely out of the wings before he was gone again—more a prompter's whisper than a recognizable face in the cast.

The slave's first appearance occurred in a short article by the scholar E. Strauss, in the 1942 issue of a Hebrew journal, *Zion*, published in Jerusalem. The article bore the title 'New Sources for the History of Middle Eastern Jews' and it contained transcriptions of several medieval documents. Among them was a letter written by a merchant living in Aden—that port which sits, like a fly on a funnel, on the precise point where the narrow spout of the Red Sea opens into the Indian Ocean. The letter, which now bears the catalogue number MS H.6, of the National and University Library in Jerusalem, was written by a merchant called Khalaf ibn Isḥaq, and it was intended for a friend of his, who bore the name Abraham Ben Yijû. The address, written on the back of the letter, shows that Ben Yiju was then living in Mangalore—a port on the south-western coast of India. In Strauss's estimation, the letter was written in the summer of 1148AD.

In the summer of its writing, Palestine was a thoroughfare for European armies. A German army had arrived in April, led by the ageing King Conrad III of Hohenstaufen, known as Almân to the Arabs. Accompanying the king was his nephew, the young and charismatic Frederick of Swabia. The Germans struck fear into the local population. 'That year the German Franks arrived,' wrote an Arab historian, 'a particularly fearsome kind of Frank.' Soon afterwards, King Louis VII of France visited Jerusalem with his army and a retinue of nobles. Travelling with him was his wife, the captivating Eleanor of Aquitaine, the greatest heiress in Europe, and destined to be successively Queen of France and England.

It was a busy season in Palestine. On 24 June a great concourse of the crowned heads of Europe gathered near Acre, in Galilee. They were received by King Baldwin and Queen Melisende of Jerusalem, with their leading barons and prelates, as well as the Grand Masters of the Orders of the Temple and the Hospital. King Conrad was accompanied by his kinsmen, Henry Jasimirgott of Austria, Otto of Freisingen, Frederick of Swabia, Duke Welf of Bavaria, and by the margraves of Verona and Montferrat. Among the nobles accompanying the King and Queen of France were Robert of Dreux, Henry of Champagne, and Thierry, Count of Flanders.

Between festivities, the leaders of the crusading armies held meetings to deliberate on their strategy for the immediate future. 'There was a divergence of views amongst them,' their enemies noted, 'but at length they came to an agreed decision to attack the city of Damascus...' For the Muslim rulers of Jordan and Syria, who had only just begun to recover from the first hundred years of the Crusades, this was a stroke of unexpected good fortune because Damascus was at that time the only Muslim state in the region that had friendly relations with the Crusader kingdoms.

On 24 July 1148AD the greatest Crusader army ever assembled camped in the orchards around Damascus. Its leaders had some successes over the next couple of days, but the Damascenes fought back with fierce determination and soon enough the Crusaders were forced to pack up camp. But Turcoman horsemen hung upon their flanks as they withdrew, raining down arrows, and the retreat rapidly turned into a rout. After this battle 'the German Franks returned' wrote the Arab historian who had so dreaded their arrival, 'to their country which lies over yonder and God rid the faithful of this calamity.'

It was not until 1942, the very summer when Khalaf's letter slipped quietly into twentieth-century print, that the Middle East again saw so great and varied a gathering of foreigners. Nowhere were there more than in the area around Alexandria; the Afrika Corps and the Italian Sixth Army, under the command of Erwin Rommel, were encamped a bare forty miles from the city, waiting for their orders for the final push into Egypt, and in the city itself the soldiers of the British Eighth Army were still arriving—from every corner of the world: India, Australia, South Africa, Britain and America. That summer, while the fates of the two armies hung in the balance, Alexandria was witness to the last, most spectacular, burst of cosmopolitan gaiety for which the city was once famous.

WITHIN THIS TORNADO of grand designs and historical destinies, Khalaf ibn Ishaq's letter seems to open a trapdoor into a vast network of foxholes where real life continues uninterrupted. Khalaf was probably well aware of the events taking place farther north: the city he lived in, Aden, served as one of the principal conduits in the flow of trade between the Mediterranean and the Indian Ocean, and Khalaf and his fellow merchants had a wide network of contacts all over North Africa, the Middle East and southern Europe. They made it their business to keep themselves well-informed: from season to season they followed the fluctuations of the prices of iron, pepper and cardamom in the markets of Cairo. They were always quick to relay news to their friends, wherever they happened to be, and they are sure to have kept themselves well abreast of the happenings in Syria and Palestine.

But now, in the summer of 1148, writing to Abraham Ben Yiju in Mangalore, Khalaf spends no time on the events up north. He begins by giving his friend news of his brother Mubashshir (who has set off unexpectedly for Syria), letting him know that he is well. Then he switches to business: he acknowledges certain goods he has received from Ben Yiju—a shipment of areca nuts, two locks manufactured in India and two bowls from a brass factory in which Ben Yiju has an interest. He informs Ben Yiju that he is sending him some presents with the letter—'things which have no price and no value.' The list seems to hint at a sweet tooth in Ben Yiju: 'two jars of sugar, a jar of almonds and two jars of raisins, altogether five jars.'

It is only at the very end of the letter that the slave makes his entry: Khalaf ibn Ishaq makes a point of singling him out and sending him 'plentiful greetings.'

That is all: no more than a name and a greeting. But the reference comes to us from a moment in time when the only people for whom we can even begin to imagine properly human, individual, existences are the literate and the consequential, the wazirs and the sultans, the chroniclers and the priests—the people who had the power to inscribe themselves physically upon time. But the slave of Khalaf's letter was not of that company: in his instance it was a mere accident that those barely discernible traces that ordinary people leave upon the world happen to have been preserved. It is nothing less than a miracle that anything is known about him at all.

THIRTY-ONE YEARS were to pass before the modern world again caught a glimpse of the slave of MS H.6: the so-called Yom Kippur War was just over and the price of oil had risen 370 per cent in the course of a single year.

The Slave's second appearance, like his first, occurs in a letter by Khalaf ibn Ishaq, written in Aden—one that happened to be included in a collection entitled *Letters of Medieval Jewish Traders*, translated and edited by Professor S. D. Goitein, of Princeton University. Like the other letter, this one too is addressed to Abraham Ben Yiju, in Mangalore, but in the thirty-one years that have passed between the publication of the one and the other, the Slave has slipped backwards in time, like an awkward package on a conveyor belt. He is nine years younger—the letter in which his name now appears was written by Khalaf ibn Ishaq in 1139.

This is another eventful year in the Middle East: the atabeg of Damascus has been assassinated and the Levant is riven by wars between Muslim principalities. But as ever Khalaf, in Aden, is unconcerned by politics; now, even more than in the other letter, business weighs heavily on his mind. A consignment of Indian pepper in which he and Ben Yiju had invested jointly has been lost in a shipwreck off the narrow straits that lead into the Red Sea. The currents there are notoriously treacherous; they have earned the Straits a dismal name, Bab al-Mandab, 'the Gateway of Lamentation'. Divers have salvaged a few pieces of iron, little else. In the meanwhile a shipment of cardamom sent by Ben Yiju has been received in Aden, and a cargo of silk dispatched in return. There are also accounts for a long list of household goods that Ben Yiju has asked for, complete with an apology for the misadventures of a frying-pan—'You asked me to buy a frying-pan of stone in a case. Later on, its case broke, whereupon I bought you an iron pan for a niṣâfî, which is, after all, better than a stone pan.'

Yet, despite all the merchandise it speaks of, the letter's spirit is anything but mercenary: it is lit with a warmth that Goitein's translation renders still alive and glowing, in cold English print. 'I was glad,' writes Khalaf ibn Ishaq 'when I looked at your letter, even before I had taken notice of its contents. Then I read it, full of happiness and, while studying it, became joyous and cheerful...You mentioned, my master, that you were longing for me. Believe me that I feel twice as strongly and even more than what you have described...'

Again the Slave's entry occurs towards the end of the main body of the text; again Khalaf sends him 'plentiful greetings' mentioning him by name. The Slave's role is no less brief upon his second appearance than it was in his first. But he has grown in stature now: he has earned himself a footnote.

The footnote is very brief. It merely explains him as Ben Yiju's Indian 'slave and business agent, a respected member of his household.'

The letter is prefaced with a few sentences about Ben Yiju. They describe him as a Jewish merchant, originally of Tunisia, who had gone to India by way of Egypt, as a trader, and had spent seventeen years there. A man of many accomplishments, a distinguished calligrapher, scholar and poet, Ben Yiju had returned to Egypt having amassed great wealth in India. The last years of his life were spent in Egypt, and his papers found their way into his synagogue in Cairo: they were eventually discovered in a chamber known as the Geniza.

I CAME UPON Professor Goitein's book of translations in a library in Oxford in the winter of 1978. I was a student, twenty-two years old, and I had recently won a scholarship awarded by a foundation established by a family of expatriate Indians. It was only a few months since I had left India and so I was perhaps a little more befuddled by my situation than students usually are. At that moment the only thing I knew about my future was that I was expected to do research leading towards a doctorate in social anthropology. I had never heard of the Cairo Geniza before that day, but within a few months I was in Tunisia, learning Arabic. At about the same time the next year, 1980, I was in Egypt, installed in a village called Laṭaîfa, a couple of hours journey to the south-east of Alexandria.

I knew nothing then about the Slave of MS H.6 except that he had given me a right to be there, a sense of entitlement.

LAṬAÎFA

1

I FIRST BEGAN to dream of Cairo in the evenings, as I sat in my room, listening, while Abu-ʻAli berated his wife or shouted at some unfortunate customer who had happened to incur his displeasure while making purchases at his shop. I would try to shut out the noise by concentrating on my book or my diaries or by turning up the volume of my transistor radio, but Abu-ʻAli's voice always prevailed, despite the thick mud walls of his house and the squawking of the ducks and geese who lived around my room.

Nobody in Lataifa liked Abu-ʻAli; neither his relatives, nor his neighbours nor anyone else in the hamlet—not even, possibly, his own wife and children. Some actively hated him; others merely tried to keep out of his way. It was hard to do otherwise; he was profoundly unlovable.

Still, dislike him as they might, Abu-ʻAli's neighbours and kinsmen also held him in fear. The children of the hamlet were always careful to be discreet when they mimicked him: they would look up and down the lanes to make sure that neither he nor his burly eldest son, ʻAli, were in sight, and then, screwing up their faces in imitation of his scowl, making imaginary sunglasses out of their fingers and thumbs, they would arch their backs and stagger down the lane, labouring under the weight of gigantic bellies.

Everybody in the area knew of Abu-'Ali's temper and most people did their best to avoid him, so far as they could. As for me, I had no choice in the matter: by the time I had learnt of Abu-'Ali's reputation, I was already his lodger, and he, on his own initiative, had assumed the role of surrogate father as well as landlord.

I was not the first person in the hamlet to find himself thrust into an unwelcome proximity with Abu-'Ali. It so happened that his house sat astride the one major road in the area, a narrow, rutted dirt track just about wide enough to allow two lightweight vehicles to squeeze past each other without toppling into the canal that ran beside it. The road served a large network of villages around Lataifa and a ragged procession of pick-up trucks roared up and down it all day long, carrying people back and forth from Damanhour, the capital of the Governorate and the largest city in the region.

Abu-'Ali's house was so placed that it commanded a good view of the road and, being the man he was, Abu-'Ali was diligent in exploiting the strategic potential of its location. He spent much of his time on a small veranda at the front of his house, lying on a divan and keeping a careful eye on the traffic. At the busier times of the day, he would lie on his side, with one arm resting voluptuously on the gigantic swell of his hip, watching the passing trucks through a pair of silver-tipped sunglasses; in the afternoons, once he had eaten his lunch, he would roll on his back and doze, his eyes half-shut, like an engorged python stealing a rest after its monthly meal.

One of the elders of the hamlet, Shaikh Musa, told me once,

when I was having dinner at his house, that Abu-'Ali had always been obese, even as a boy. He had never been able to work in the fields because he had hurt his leg as a child, and had soon grown much heavier than others of his age. People had felt sorry for him to begin with, but later the injury had proved such an advantage that everyone had begun to wonder about its authenticity: it had given him an excuse for not working on the land and as a result his father had allowed him to go through school. Nothing was heard of his injury thereafter. Later, he'd even gone on to college in Damanhour, which was unusual at the time for a fellah boy, the son of an unlettered peasant. Sure enough, he had seen to it that his time in college was well spent: he had cultivated contacts with students from influential families, and with bureaucrats and officials in Damanhour. It hadn't surprised anyone when he succeeded in getting a permit to set up a government-subsidized shop for retailing essential commodities at controlled prices.

That permit was to become Abu-'Ali's passport to prosperity: his was the only shop of its kind in the area (he had made sure of that) and everybody had to go to him if they wanted to buy sugar, tea, oil and suchlike at government-subsidized prices. Often his customers were more supplicants than patrons, for there was nothing to prevent him from choosing whom to sell to: people who got on the wrong side of him frequently discovered that he was out of tea or kerosene or whatever it was they wanted. It was all the same to Abu-'Ali: he had no shortage of customers—they had to come to him or go all the way to the next village, Nashâwy, a mile and a half down the road.

It was thus that Abu-'Ali had grown so large, Shaikh Musa said (he was generally extremely reluctant to discuss Abu-'Ali but on this occasion he permitted himself a laugh): for years he had eaten meat like other people ate beans, and eventually he had swollen up like one of the force-fed geese his wife reared on their roof.

'Women use their forefingers to push corn down the throats of their geese,' added Shaikh Musa's son Ahmed, an earnest young man, who was a great deal more heedful of my duties as a gatherer of information than I. 'Corn, as you ought to know, is harvested just before winter, towards the start of the Coptic year which begins in the month of Tût...'

It had long been a point of pride with Abu-'Ali that he possessed more—more gadgets, especially—than anyone else in Lataifa. It was therefore a matter of bitter chagrin to him that he had not been the first person in the village to buy a television set. One of his own half-brothers, a schoolteacher, had beaten him to it.

He was often reminded of this by a cousin's son, Jabir, a boy in his late teens, with bright, malicious eyes and a tongue that bristled with barbs. Sometimes, when we were sitting in Abu-'Ali's guest-room in the evenings, Jabir would turn to me and ask questions like 'What's the name of the captain of the Algerian soccer team?' or 'Who is the Raïs of India? Isn't it Indira Gandhi?' The questions were entirely rhetorical; he would answer them himself, and then, sighing with pleasure he would glance at his uncle and exclaim: 'Oh there's so much to be learnt from television. It's lucky for us there's one next door.'

It always worked.

'I don't understand this television business,' Abu-'Ali would roar. 'What's the point of buying a television set now, when our village doesn't even have electricity?'

Smiling serenely, Jabir would point out that a television set could be run perfectly well on car batteries.

'Car batteries!' Abu-'Ali's voice would be breathy with contempt. 'That's like burning up money. I'm telling you, and you pay attention, let the electricity come to Lataifa as the government's promised, and you'll be able to watch the biggest and best TV set you've ever seen, right here, in this room, God willing. It'll be better than the best television set in Nashawy, insha'allah, and it'll be in colour too.'

A sly smile would appear on Jabir's blunt-featured face, with its adolescent's crop of stubble and unquiet skin. 'There'll be other colour TVs here soon,' he would say, leaning back contentedly against the bolsters on the couch. 'My uncle Mustafa is going to get one for our house any one of these days, insha'allah.'

All Abu-'Ali could do in retaliation was glare at him; he knew he was no match for Jabir's tongue. He would have loved to ban Jabir from his house, but it so happened that Jabir's father was a cousin in the paternal line, and thus a member of the extended family, or lineage, of which Abu-'Ali was nominally the head: he couldn't have thrown Jabir out of his house without offending a whole platoon of relatives. Besides, it so happened that Jabir was also best friends with one of Abu-'Ali's sons, a schoolboy of his own age, about sixteen or so. The two of them were always together, with their arms around each others' shoulders, giggling, or talking in furtive, experimental whispers. There was little Abu-'Ali could do to rid his house of him; constrained as he was by the obligations of kinship, he had to choke daily on the gall of hearing about the soccer matches that his son and Jabir watched on the TV set in the house next door.

'What's in this soccer stuff, I want to know?' Abu-'Ali would explode from time to time. 'Isn't there work to do? Allah! Is the world going to live on soccer? What's going to become of...'

But laggardly though he may have been in the matter of television, Abu-'Ali was undeniably the first person in the hamlet to acquire a form of motorized transport—a light Japanese moped, fragile in appearance, but extraordinarily sturdy in build. The moped was normally used by one of his older sons, who drove it to his college in Damanhour every day. He was very jealous of his custodianship of the vehicle and would never allow his brothers or cousins to use it—but his father, of course, was another matter altogether.

Every now and again, Abu-'Ali would roll off his divan, send his wife in to fetch his best dark glasses, and shout for the moped to be wheeled out into the courtyard. He would hitch up the hem of his jallabeyya and then, lifting up his leg, he would mount the vehicle with a little sidelong hop, while his son held it steady. To me, watching from the roof, it seemed hardly credible that so delicate a machine would succeed in carrying a man of Abu-'Ali's weight over that bumpy dirt track. But to my astonishment it invariably did: he would go shooting off down the road, his jallabeyya ballooning out around him, while the moped, in profile, diminished into a thin, sharp line—it was like watching a gargantuan lollipop being carried away by its stick.

It was no accident that Abu-'Ali had acquired so many possessions: everyone agreed that he had a remarkable talent for squeezing the last piastre from everything that came his way. People often said that it was useless to bargain with Abu-'Ali: in the end he would get exactly what he wanted.

I was soon to discover the truth of this for myself.

One afternoon, about a month or so after I had arrived in Lataifa, Abu-'Ali came up to my room to pay me a visit. This was an unusual event because it called for the climbing of a narrow flight of stairs. I lived on the roof of his house, in an old chicken-coop, which his wife had once used for her poultry. Her stock of ducks, chickens, pigeons and geese had been moved to a pen, at the far end of the roof, and the coop had been turned into a makeshift room for my benefit, with a bed, a desk and a chair.

I had discovered since moving in that an afternoon visit from Abu-'Ali was generally good cause for apprehension. At that time of the day he was normally to be found lying inert upon his divan, resting after his midday meal; it was unusual for him to so much as turn on his side, much less attempt an assault on the stairs that led to the roof. He had only visited me twice before in the afternoon, and on both occasions it was because he had wanted a discussion in private, while his children were away at work or in school. On one of those occasions he had tried to lay claim to my transistor radio, my best-loved possession, and on the other he had indicated, after a prolonged and roundabout conversation, that the rent I was paying was not satisfactory and that either I or the 'doktór' who had brought me to his house would have to do something about it.

I had been brought to Abu-'Ali's house by Doctor Aly Issa, Professor in the University of Alexandria, and one of the most eminent anthropologists in the Middle East. An acquaintance of Doctor Issa's had led us to Abu-'Ali, who had declaimed: 'I swear to you, ya doktór, the Indian shall stay here and we will look after him as we do our own sons, for your sake, ya doktór, because we respect you so much.'

Being the kindest and most generous of men, Doctor Issa had all too easily allowed himself to take Abu-'Ali at his word. It had been agreed upon very quickly—all except how much I was to pay. The Professor had brushed aside my anxiety on that score:

'That will be easily settled, I will write him a letter—don't worry about it.'

And so he had, but Abu-'Ali had seen little merit in Doctor Issa's letter. Now, having settled himself on my bed, he took the dog-eared letter out of the pocket of his jallabeyya once again, and read it through, clicking his tongue and frowning.

'Tell me,' he said at last, 'where did you stay while you were in Alexandria?'

'A small hotel,' I answered.

'And how much did it cost?'

'Two pounds a night.'

He gave a little nod of satisfaction and put the letter away. 'Hotels are expensive,' he said, 'you're lucky to be staying here with us. We will cook for you, wash your clothes for you, provide you with anything you need. You must ask for whatever you want whenever you want it. To us you are just like our sons—why we will even give you our own money if you like.'

He reached into his pocket for his wallet and held it out to me, smiling, his eyes vanishing into the folds of his immense, fleshy face. 'You can take this,' he said. 'You can have our money.'

I stared at the wallet, mesmerized, wondering whether custom demanded that I touch it or make some other symbolic gesture of acceptance or obeisance, like falling at his feet. I saw myself shrinking, dwindling away into one of those tiny, terrified foreigners whom Pharaohs hold up by their hair in New Kingdom bas-reliefs.

But the wallet vanished back into his pocket in a flash, before I had time to respond. 'You see,' he said, 'that is how much we love you.'

'I was just thinking,' I stammered, at last, 'maybe I could buy my own food.'

'How can you do that?' he responded indignantly. 'The shops are far away, and you know it would cost you at least a pound a day if you were to buy your food in town. No, no, you must eat with us.'

'No, I meant, I could give you the money...' My Arabic had begun to falter now under the strain of bargaining, and I was slowly sinking into a tongue-tied silence.

'No, no, it's not a question of money. You are our honoured guest. You can see that I don't care for money. I have a big shop downstairs, and I sell many things there. Next year I will add a second floor to my house, insha'allah. You know I have sent my sons to school and college; you can see that I don't care for money at all.'

'Please tell me,' I said, 'how much do you think I should pay?'

He sighed thoughtfully, rubbing his moustache.

'No,' he said, 'you must tell us how much you would like to give us.'

And so it went on for a good hour or so, before he would allow himself to be cajoled into naming a sum.

That evening, at sunset, I was standing on the roof, looking out over the tranquil, twilit cottonfields, when Abu-'Ali's voice exploded out of the porch below, roaring abuse at his wife. I went back into my room and in an effort to shut out the noise, I began to turn the dial on my radio, scanning the waves for the sound of a familiar language, listening for words that would make me feel a little less alone. As the night wore on, the thought of hearing Abu-'Ali's voice for months on end, perhaps years, began to seem utterly intolerable.

It was on nights like that that my dreams of Cairo were most vivid.

2

CAIRO IS EGYPT'S own metaphor for itself.

Everywhere in the country except the city itself, Cairo *is* Egypt. They are both spoken of by the same name, Maṣr, a name that is appropriate as well as ancient, a derivative of a root that means 'to settle' or 'to civilize'. The word has a long history in Arabic; it occurs in the Qur'ân but was in use even before the advent of Islam. It is the name by which the country has been known, in its own language, for at least a millennium, and most of the cultures and civilizations with which it has old connections have accepted its own self-definition. The languages of India, for example, know Masr by variations of its Arabic name: 'Mishor' in Bengali, 'Misar' in Hindi and Urdu. Only Europe has always insisted on knowing the country not on its own terms, but as a dark mirror for itself. 'Egyptian darkness,' says the Oxford English Dictionary, quoting the Bible, 'intense darkness (see Exodus x.22).' Or 'Egyptian days: the two days in each month which were believed to be unlucky'; and: 'Egyptian bondage: bondage like that of the Israelites in Egypt.'

Like English, every major European language derives its name for Egypt from the Greek Ægyptos, a term that is related to the word 'Copt', the name generally used for Egypt's indigenous Christians. Thus German has its Ägypten, Dutch Egypte, Polish and Estonian Egipt: old resonant words, with connotations and histories far in excess of those that usually attach to the names of countries. A seventeenth-century English law, for example, states: 'If any transport into England or Wales, any lewd people calling themselves Egyptians, they forfeit 40 £'—a reminder that words like 'gypsy' and 'gitano' derived from 'Egyptian'.

Europe's apparently innocent 'Egypt' is therefore as much a metaphor as 'Masr', but a less benign one, almost as much a weapon as a word. Egypt's own metaphor for itself, on the other hand, renders the city indistinguishable from the country; a usage that brims with pleasing and unexpected symmetries.

Like Egypt, Cairo dwindles into a thin ribbon of settlements at its southern extremity; towards the north it gradually broadens, like the country itself, into a wide, densely populated funnel. To the south lies Upper Egypt, the Ṣaʿîd, a long thin carpet of green that flanks the Nile on both sides; to the north is the triangle created by the river, as perfect as any in Nature, the Delta. Egypt's metaphor, Egypt itself, sits in between like a hinge, straddling the imaginary line that since the beginning of human history has divided the country into two parts, each distinct and at the same time perfectly complementary.

To most Egyptians outside Cairo, their metaphor stands for the entire city: the whole of it is known as Masr—the city's formal name al-Qâhira is infrequently used. But Cairo, like Delhi or Rome, is actually not so much a single city as an archipelago of townships, founded on neighbouring sites, by various different dynasties and rulers.

When the people of Cairo speak of Masr, they often have a particular district of the city in mind. It lies towards the south, and it goes by several names. Sometimes it is spoken of as Old Cairo, Maṣr al-Qadîma or Maṣr al-ʿAtîqa, sometimes as Mari Gargis, but most often as Fusṭâṭ Maṣr, or simply Fusṭâṭ. On a map, the quarter seems very small, far too small to be so rich in names. But in fact, small as it is, the area is not a single island within Cairo, but rather a second archipelago within the first.

It was a small enclave within this formation that eventually became home to Abraham Ben Yiju, the master of the Slave of MS H.6: a Roman fortress called Babylon. The fort was built by the emperor Trajan in 130AD, on the site of an even earlier structure, and the Romans are said to have called it Babylon of Egypt, to distinguish it from the Mesopotamian Babylon. The name may have come from the Arabic Bâb il-On, 'The Gate of On', after the ancient sanctuary of the Sun God at Heliopolis, but there are many contending theories and no one knows for sure. The fort has had other names, most notably Qaṣr al-Shamaʿ, Fortress of the Lamp, but it is Babylon that has served it longest.

The entrance to Babylon was once guarded by two massive, heavily buttressed towers: one of them is now a ruined stump, and the other was incorporated several centuries ago into the structure of a Greek Orthodox church. Today the towers, and the gateway that lies between them, are separated from the Nile by several hundred metres. But at the time when the fortress was built the river flowed directly beside it: the reason why the towers were so solidly constructed is that they served as Babylon's principal embankment against the annual Nile flood. In the early years of Babylon's history, the towers were flanked by a port. As the centuries advanced and the conurbation around the fortress grew in size and importance, the river retreated westwards and the docks and warehouses gradually expanded along the newly emerged lands on the bank. In Ben Yiju's time the port was one of the busiest in the Middle East; it was said to handle more traffic than Baghdad and Basra combined.

Today there is a steel gate between Babylon's twin towers, and millions of visitors pour through it every year. But the fort's second great gateway, in its southern wall, is no longer in use: its floor is deep in water now, swamped by Cairo's rapidly rising water-table. A thick film of green slime shimmers within its soaring, vaulted interior, encircling old tyres and discarded plastic bottles. Incredible as it may seem, this putrefying pit marks the site of what was perhaps the single most important event in the history of Cairo, indeed of Egypt: it was through this gateway that the Arab general 'Amr ibn al-'Âṣ is thought to have effected his entry into Babylon in 641AD—the decisive event in the futûḥ, the Muslim victory over the Christian powers in Masr.

For Babylon, ironically, the moment of capitulation marked its greatest triumph for it was then that this tiny fortress fixed the location of the country's centre of gravity, once and for all. It was Alexandria that was Egypt's most important city at the time of the Arab invasion; founded by Alexander the Great in 332BC it had served as the country's capital for almost a thousand years. Babylon, on the other hand, was a mere provincial garrison, a small military outpost. By rights therefore, it was Alexandria's prerogative to serve as the funnel for the assimilation of the newcomers.

But the conquering Muslim general, 'Amr ibn al-'As, broke with the usual practice of invaders by electing to base his army not in the country's capital, but in an entirely new city. The location he chose was the obvious one—the site the Arab army had used for its camp while laying siege to Babylon. The fortress was thus the promontory that served to anchor the Cairo archipelago: ever afterwards Egypt's capital, Masr, Egypt's metaphor for itself, has lain within a few miles of Babylon.

The legend goes that on the morning when 'Amr was to lead his army against Alexandria he woke to find a dove nesting on top of his tent. Loath to invite misfortune by disturbing the bird, he left the tent behind and upon returning to Babylon after his successful assault on Alexandria, laid out his new city around the nest-topped tent. The legend is universally believed in Cairo, and everyone who repeats it adds that the name of 'Amr's city, al-Fusṭāṭ, was derived from the Arabic for tent. But in fact the story came into circulation long after the event and is almost certainly apocryphal. It is possible that the name does not come from an Arabic source at all, being related instead to the Latin-Greek word 'fossaton', which is also the parent of an archaic and unglamorous English word, 'fosse', or ditch.

Fustat served as Egypt's capital for more than three centuries, but then a new invasion and a new set of conquerors moved the centre of power a couple of miles northwards. The new rulers were the Fatimids, a dynasty which had its beginnings in North Africa, in an esoteric Shî'a sect whose members were known as Ismâ'îlîs. In 969AD one of their generals, a former Greek slave called Jawhar al-Rûmî, marched against Egypt with a hundred thousand men. Their army routed the Egyptians in a battle near Fustat and the inhabitants of the city soon sued for peace. Like 'Amr ibn al-'As before him, Jawhar the Greek marked out the boundaries of a new township right beside the conquered city. Soothsayers are said to have named the town al-Qâhira, the Martial, or the Victorious, because the planet Mars, al-Qâhir, was in the ascendant at the time of the foundation ceremony. It was this name that was to pass into European languages as Cairo, Le Caire and the like.

In its original conception al-Qahira was a planned capital, an early forebear of New Delhi, Canberra, Brasilia and other such haunts of officialdom. The Caliph had his residence there and it contained many notable buildings, but everything in it was the personal property of the rulers and its shops and bazaars existed only to serve him and his entourage. In time the character of al-Qahira was to change entirely and it was to become a frantic, crowded district, the bustling nucleus of the conurbation of Cairo. But all that came later: in the early years of the twelfth century when Ben Yiju first came to Masr it was probably still a relatively solemn, bureaucratic kind of place. At the time, the Fatimids, who had long since embarked on a course of catastrophic decline, were clinging to the last tatters of their power, and their capital was still largely a ceremonial and administrative township. It was Fustat then that probably had something of the busy, market-place character of al-Qahira today.

Thriving hub though it was, medieval Fustat probably presented an unremarkable kind of appearance. Archæological excavations have shown that its dwellings were, for the most part, made of the material that is still most in evidence in rural Egypt today, dried mud and straw—a substance that sounds somehow more glamorous when spoken of by the term 'adobe', a term appropriately applied here, since the word probably derives from the Arabic al-ṭûb, 'the brick'. Possibly Fustat even had something of the distinctive look of an Egyptian village: that tousled, mop-haired appearance that is characteristic of fellah houses, with great ricks of straw and firewood piled high on their roofs.

But in fact there was nothing remotely rustic about medieval Fustat, whatever its appearance. With the political ascendancy of the Fatimid Empire, it had come to play a pivotal role in the global economy as the entrepôt that linked the Mediterranean and the Indian Ocean: the merchandise that flowed through its bazaars came from as far afield as East Africa, southern Europe, the western Sahara, India, China and Indonesia. By Ben Yiju's time Fustat had long since become the largest island in the emerging archipelago of Masr: the juncture of some of the most important trade routes in the known world and the nucleus of one of the richest and most cosmopolitan cities on earth.

But although it may have been Fustat's markets that first attracted Ben Yiju to Masr it was Babylon that was to become his spiritual home there. The fortress had remained relatively unchanged over several centuries and was still largely populated by Christians of various denominations, with Copts in the majority. But there were also at least three Jewish groups in Babylon, each with a synagogue of its own—they were the 'Iraqis', the 'Palestinians' and the Karaites. The 'Palestinian' congregation followed the rites of the school of Jerusalem, and despite its name, it included the indigenous Jews of Egypt. It was the Palestinian synagogue that Ben Yiju was to join.

By the time Ben Yiju came to Masr, Babylon had long since been eclipsed by the thriving township of Fustat. But in the end it was the hardy little fortress that proved to have the greater staying power. Today, the entrance to what remains of Fustat lies a short distance from Babylon's towers, but very few tourists pass through it. Fustat can be smelt before it is seen—it is a gigantic open refuse-pit, an immense rubbish-dump.

The site is guarded by a large steel gate which looks as though it belongs in a prison. But it swings open easily enough, with a push, and a dusty path curls away from it, between the mounds of refuse, towards a stretch of reed-filled marshland in the distance. In places, where the decomposing matter has caught fire spontaneously under the fierce glare of the Cairo sun, thin tendrils of smoke spiral torpidly towards the sky. Children play in puddles of grey ooze and a few figures in torn, flapping jallabeyyas move slowly through the refuse, dragging piles of cardboard and plastic behind them. Incredible as it may seem, excavations in this suppurating wasteland have yielded huge quantities of Chinese pottery and other riches: it was here that some of the earliest and most valuable fragments of Indian textiles have been found.

The last skeletal remains of the city whose markets once traded in the best the world could offer lie a little further along the path: the outlines of a few foundations and some brick walls and arches, pushing through pools of oily slime, clawing at the earth. In the distance shanties grow in tiers upon the ruins, and they in turn fade gently, imperceptibly, into the scraggy geometry of Cairo's skyline—into a tableau of decay and regeneration, a metaphor for Masr.

3

I OFTEN THOUGHT of telling Shaikh Musa that I wanted to move out of Abu-'Ali's house; for a while I even considered asking him to help me make some other arrangement. I had always felt secure in his friendship, from the moment of our first meeting: there was a gentleness and a good humour about him that inspired trust, something about the way he rocked his short, portly frame from side to side as we talked, the way he shook my hand every time we met, his round, weathered face crinkling into a smile, and cried: 'Where have you been all this while? Why haven't you come to see me?'

There were times when I had the distinct impression that Shaikh Musa was trying to warn me about Abu-'Ali. The two of them were of the same age after all, in their mid-fifties; they had grown up together, and Shaikh Musa probably knew him as well as anyone in the hamlet. Once, while dining with Shaikh Musa and his family, I had the feeling that he was cautioning me, in an oblique and roundabout way, telling me to be careful with Abu-'Ali. It was only because of a series of unfortunate interruptions that I didn't beg him right then to find me some other house to live in.

We were sitting in his bedroom that evening. Shaikh Musa, his son Ahmed, his two grandsons and I were eating out of one tray, while the women of the household were sharing another, at the other end of the room. It was something of a special occasion for I had just crossed an invisible barrier. Whenever I had eaten at Shaikh Musa's house before, it had been in the 'mandara', the guest-room on the outside of the house, facing the lane; every house had one, for this was the room where male guests were usually received. But on this occasion, after saying his evening prayers, Shaikh Musa had risen to his feet and led me out of the guest-room, into the lamplit interior of the house.

We had gone directly to his bedroom, pushing past a nuzzling sheep tethered by the door. Shaikh Musa chased a brood of chickens off an old sheepskin, sending them scuttling under his bed, and we seated ourselves on the floor and played with Ahmed's two young sons while waiting for the rest of the family. After Ahmed returned from the mosque, two women came into the room carrying a pair of trays loaded with food. The trays were set out on the floor, and the women gathered around one, while we seated ourselves at the other; each tray was as big as a cartwheel, and there was plenty of room for all of us.

There were three women in the room now, all of them young, one in the first bloom of her adolescence with a gentle, innocent face and a rosy complexion—a family inheritance shared by many of the inhabitants of Lataifa. From the strong resemblance she bore to Ahmed, I knew at once that she was his sister. The other two women were a good deal older, perhaps in their mid-twenties. One was a pale, pretty, self-possessed young woman, dressed in a long, printed skirt. The other was dark and thick-set, and she was wearing a black fuṣṭân, a heavy, shapeless robe that was the customary garb of a fellah woman.

I had encountered all of them before, occasionally at the doorway to Shaikh Musa's house and sometimes in the guest-room when they came in to hand out tea. There were times when I had the impression that I had passed them in the lanes of the hamlet, but I was never quite sure. The fault for this lay entirely with me, for neither they nor anyone else in Lataifa wore veils (nor indeed did anyone in the region), but at that time, early in my stay, I was so cowed by everything I had read about Arab traditions of shame and modesty that I barely glanced at them, for fear of giving offence. Later it was I who was shame-stricken, thinking of the astonishment and laughter I must have provoked, walking past them, eyes lowered, never uttering so much as a word of greeting. Shaking hands with them now, as we sat down to dinner, I tried to work out the connections between them and the rest of the family. The pretty woman in the printed dress was Ahmed's wife, I decided: her clothes and her bearing spoke of a college, or at least a high-school, education. Since Ahmed had been through school and college too, I had every reason to assume that they were a couple. As for the other woman, the dark one in the black dress, it took me no more than a moment's thought to reach a conclusion about her: she was the wife of Shaikh Musa's other son, I decided, Ahmed's younger brother, Hasan.

I had never met Hasan, for he was away, serving his draft in the army, but I had heard a great deal about him. Shaikh Musa spoke of him often, and with something more than the usual warmth of a father remembering a son long absent. He had shown me a picture of him once: he was a strikingly good-looking young man, with a broad, strong face and clear-cut features; in fact, he bore a marked resemblance to a picture of Shaikh Musa that hung on the wall of his guest-room, a photograph taken in his youth, in army uniform.

Unlike Ahmed, who had been through school and college, Hasan had not had an education. He had been taken out of school at a fairly early age; Shaikh Musa had brought him up as a fellah, so that at least one of his sons would profit from the land their ancestors had left them. It was that shared background perhaps that lent Shaikh Musa's voice a special note of affection when he spoke of Hasan: Ahmed was the most dutiful of sons and he helped Shaikh Musa on the land as often as he could, but there was an unbridgeable gap between them now because of his education. Ahmed worked as a clerk, in a factory near Damanhour, and he was thus counted as a mowazzaf, an educated, salaried man, and like all such people in the village, his clothes, his speech, his amusements and concerns, were markedly different from those of the fellaheen. Hasan, on the other hand, fell on his father's side of that divide, and it was easy to see that their shared view of the world formed a special bond between them.

I was soon sure that the woman in the black dress was Hasan's wife. I overheard Shaikh Musa saying a few words to her and, detecting a note of familiarity in his voice, I attributed it to his special closeness to his younger son. But now I began to wonder where his own wife was and why she had not joined us at our meal.

The meal that was set out on the tray in front of us was a very good one: arranged around a large pile of rice were dishes of fried potatoes, cheese preserved in brine, salads of chopped tomatoes and fresh dill, plates of cooked vegetables, large discs of corn-meal bread, and bowls of young Nile perch, baked with tomatoes and garlic. Everything was fresh and full of flavour, touched with that unnameable quality which makes anything grown in the soil of Egypt taste richer, more distinctively of itself, than it does anywhere else.

It was when I complimented him on the food that Shaikh Musa suddenly raised his head, as though a thought had just struck him.

'Things are cheap in the countryside,' he said, 'much cheaper than they are in the city. In the city people have to buy everything in the market, for cash, but here it isn't like that; we get everything from the fields. You should not expect to pay as much here as you would in the city. This is just a little hamlet —not even a big village like Nashawy.'

I was taken aback for a moment, and then I realized that he was referring obliquely to Abu-'Ali: he had asked me once how much I paid him and had sunk into an amazed silence when I quoted the sum. But before I could say anything, Shaikh Musa changed the subject: resorting to one of his favourite ploys he began to talk about agriculture.

'And these,' he said, pointing at the cucumbers on the tray, 'are called khiyâr. The best are those that are sown early, in spring, in the month of Amshîr by the Coptic calendar.'

Not one to be left behind in a conversation of that kind,

Ahmed immediately added: 'Amshir follows the month of Ṭûba, when the earth awakes, as we say, and after it comes Barmahât...'

Later, after dinner, when Shaikh Musa and I were alone in the room for a while, he began to wax expansive, talking about his boyhood in Lataifa and about Abu-'Ali as a child. But once the family returned he cut himself short, and there was no opportunity to discuss the matter again for shortly afterwards he got up and left the room.

No sooner had Shaikh Musa left than Ahmed began to tell me how cotton was rotated with the fodder crop berseem. 'Write it down,' he said, handing me my notebook, 'or else you'll forget.'

I scribbled desultorily for a while, and then, searching desperately for something else to talk about, I happened to ask him if his mother was away from the hamlet.

A hush immediately descended upon the room. At length, Ahmed cleared his throat and said: 'My mother, God have mercy on her, died a year ago.'

There was a brief silence, and then he leaned over to me. 'Do you see Sakkina there?' he asked, gesturing at the woman in the black fustan. 'My father married her this year.'

For a moment I was speechless: in my mind Shaikh Musa was very old and very venerable, and I was oddly unsettled by the thought of his marrying a woman a fraction his age.

His wife noticed me staring and smiled shyly. Then, Ahmed's wife, the self-possessed young woman in the cotton dress, turned to me and said: 'She's heard about you from her family. You have met her uncle, haven't you? Ustaz Mustafa?'

Again I was taken completely by surprise. But now things began to fall into place.

4

JABIR, ABU-'ALI'S YOUNG relative, had woken me one morning, soon after I arrived in Lataifa. 'Get up, ya mister,' he said, shaking me. 'Get up and meet my uncle.'

I sat up bleary-eyed and found myself looking at a short, plump man who bore a strong family resemblance to Jabir; he had the same rosy complexion, blunt features and bright, black eyes. He also had a little clipped moustache, and the moment I saw it I knew it was the kind of moustache that Jabir was sure to aspire to once his feathery adolescent whiskers had matured.

At that time, I was still innocent of some of the finer distinctions between salaried people and fellaheen but I could tell at once, from his starchy blue jallabeyya and white net skull-cap, that Jabir's uncle did not make his living from ploughing the land. Jabir's introduction made things clearer, for he added the word Ustaz, 'Teacher', to his uncle's name—a title usually given to men who had been educated in modern, rather than traditional, forms of learning.

'This is Ustaz Mustafa,' said Jabir. 'My uncle. He studied law at the University of Alexandria.'

Ustaz Mustafa smiled and, nodding vigorously, he addressed me in classical, literary Arabic. 'We are honoured,' he said, 'to have Your Presence amongst us.'

I was dismayed to be spoken to in this way, for in concentrating on learning the dialect of the village I had allowed my studies of classical Arabic to fall into neglect. I stuttered, unsure of how to respond, but then, unexpectedly, Jabir came to my rescue. Clapping me on the back, he told his uncle: 'He is learning to talk just like us.'

Ustaz Mustafa's face lit up. 'Insha'allah,' he cried, 'God willing, he will soon be one of us.'

I noticed that he had a habit of flicking back the cuff of his jallabeyya every few minutes or so to steal a quick look at his watch. I was to discover later that this gesture was rooted in an anxiety that had long haunted his everyday existence: the fear that he might inadvertently miss one of the day's five required prayers. That was why he looked much busier than anyone else in Lataifa—he was always in a hurry to get to the mosque. 'I have read all about India,' said Ustaz Mustafa, smiling serenely. 'There is a lot of chilli in the food and when a man dies his wife is dragged away and burnt alive.'

'Not always,' I protested, 'my grandmother for example…'

Jabir was drinking this in, wide-eyed.

'And of course,' Ustaz Mustafa continued, 'you have Indira Gandhi, and her son Sanjay Gandhi, who used to sterilize the Muslims…'

'No, no, he sterilized everyone,' I said.

His eyes widened and I added hastily: 'No, not me of course, but…'

'Yes,' he said, nodding sagely. 'I know. I read all about India when I was in college in Alexandria.'

He had spent several years in Alexandria as a student, he said; he had specialized in civil and religious law and now practised in a court in Damanhour. He talked at length about his time at university, the room he had lived in and the books he had read, and in the meanwhile two of Abu-'Ali's sons came up to join us, carrying a tray of tea.

Soon, the conversation turned to village gossip and for a while, to my relief, I was forgotten. But Jabir was not going to allow me so easy an escape: he had noticed that Ustaz Mustafa's questions had unsettled me and he was impatient for more entertainment.

'Ask him more about his country,' he whispered to his uncle. 'Ask him about his religion.'

The reminder was superfluous for, as I later discovered, religion was a subject never very far from Ustaz Mustafa's mind. 'All right then,' he said to me, motioning to the boys to be quiet. 'Tell me, are you Muslim?'

'No,' I said, but he didn't really need an answer since everyone in the hamlet knew that already.

'So then what are you?'

'I was born a Hindu,' I said reluctantly, for if I had a religious identity at all it was largely by default.

There was a long silence during which I tried hard to think of an arresting opening line that would lead the conversation towards some bucolic, agricultural subject. But the moment passed, and in a troubled voice Ustaz Mustafa said: 'What is this "Hinduki" thing? I have heard of it before and I don't understand it. If it is not Christianity nor Judaism nor Islam what can it be? Who are its prophets?'

'It's not like that,' I said. 'There aren't any prophets...'

'So you are like the Magi?' he said, bright-eyed. 'You worship fire then?'

I shook my head vaguely, but before I could answer, he tapped my arm with his forefinger. 'No,' he said, smiling coquettishly. 'I know—it's cows you worship—isn't that so?'

There was a sharp, collective intake of breath as Jabir and the other boys recoiled, calling upon God, in whispers, to protect them from the Devil.

I cleared my throat; I knew a lot depended on my answers. 'It's not like that,' I said. 'In my country some people don't eat beef because...because cows give milk and plough the fields and so on, and so they're very useful.'

Ustaz Mustafa was not to be bought off by this spurious ecological argument. 'That can't be the reason,' he began, but then his eyes fell on his watch and a shadow of alarm descended on his face. He edged forward until he was balanced precariously on the rim of the bed.

'You still haven't told me about this "Hinduki" business,' he said. 'What is your God like?'

I tried to stutter out an answer of some kind, but fortunately for me Ustaz Mustafa wasn't really paying attention to me any more.

'Well thanks be to Allah,' he said quickly, eyeing his watch. 'Now that you are here among us you can understand and learn about Islam, and then you can make up your mind whether you want to stay within that religion of yours.'

He jumped to his feet and stretched out his hand. 'Come with me to the mosque right now,' he said. 'That is where we are going—for the noon prayers. You don't have to do anything. Just watch us pray, and soon you will understand what Islam is.'

I hesitated for a moment, and then I shook my head. 'No,' I said. 'I can't. I have many things to do.'

'Things to do?' cried Ustaz Mustafa. 'What is there to do here that you can't do later? Come with us—it's very important. Nothing could be more important.'

'No,' I said. 'I can't.'

'Why not?' he insisted quietly. 'Just come and watch—that's all I'm asking of you.'

And just then the voice of the muezzin floated over from a nearby mosque, singing the call to prayer, and before I could say another word Ustaz Mustafa and the boys had vanished from the room.

But I couldn't go back to work even after I was alone again. I began to wonder why I had not accepted Ustaz Mustafa's invitation to visit the mosque and watch him at his prayers; he had meant well, after all, had only wanted to introduce me to the most important element of his imaginative life. A part of me had wanted to go—not merely that part which told me that it was, in a sense, my duty, part of my job. But when the moment had come, I'd known that I wouldn't be able to do it: I had been too afraid, and for the life of me I could not understand why.

But soon enough, Ustaz Mustafa came back to talk to me again. This time he had a child in his arms. 'This is my son,' he said, tweaking the child's cheeks. He glowed with love as he looked at the boy.

'Say salâm to the mister,' he said, and the child, alarmed, hid his face in his father's shoulder.

Ustaz Mustafa laughed. 'I missed you the last few days,' he said to me. 'I was busy in the evenings—I had to go and meet someone in Nashawy, so I couldn't come to talk to you. But today I decided that I would come over as soon as I got back from work.'

I was better prepared for him this time, and I began to talk at length about the hamlet's history and his family's genealogy. But Ustaz Mustafa had little time for matters of that kind, and soon he began to steal anxious glances at his watch over his son's back.

Eventually he brushed my patter aside and began to ask questions, first about my family and then about Indian politics—what I thought of Indira Gandhi, was I for her or against her, and so on. Then, with a wry, derisory smile he began to ask me about 'The Man from Menoufiyya'—the current nickname for the President, the Raïs—phrasing his questions in elaborately allusive, elliptical forms, like riddles, as though he were mocking the Raïs's habit of spreading surrogate ears everywhere. My answers left him a little disappointed however, for many of his riddles had stock responses with which I was not then familiar.

Suddenly the bantering note went out of his voice.

'Tell me something,' he said, 'tell me, are you a communist?'

He used a word, shiyu'eyya, which could mean anything from 'communist' to 'atheist' and 'adulterer' in the village dialect; my understanding of it was that it referred to people who rejected all moral and ethical laws.

'No,' I said.

'All right then,' he said, 'if you're not a communist, tell me this: who made the world, and who were the first man and woman if not Âdam and Hawâ?'

I was taken aback by the abruptness of this transition. Later I came to expect elisions of this kind in conversations with people like Ustaz Mustafa, for I soon discovered that salaried people like him, rural mowazzafeen, were almost without exception absorbed in a concern which, despite its plural appearance, was actually single and indivisible—religion and politics—so that the mention of the one always led to the other. But at the time I was nonplussed. I mumbled something innocuous about how, in my country, people thought the world had always existed.

My answer made him flinch. He hugged his sleeping son hard against his chest and said, 'They don't think of Our Lord at all, do they? They live only for the present and have no thought for the hereafter.'

I began to protest but Ustaz Mustafa was not interested in my answers any more. His eyes had fallen on his watch, and he rose hurriedly to his feet. 'Tomorrow,' he said, 'I will take you with me to the graveyard, and you can watch me reciting the Quran over my father's grave. You will see then how much better Islam is than this "Hinduki" of yours.'

At the door he turned back for a moment. 'I am hoping,' he said, 'that you will convert and become a Muslim. You must not disappoint me.'

Then he was gone. A moment later I heard the distant voice of a muezzin, chanting the call to prayer.

He had meant what he said.

He came back the next evening, his Quran in his hands, and said: 'Come, let's go to the graveyard.'

'I can't,' I said quickly. 'I have to go out to the fields.'

He hesitated, and then, not without some reluctance, decided to accompany me. The truth was that walking in the fields was something of a trial for Ustaz Mustafa: it demanded ceaseless vigilance on his part to keep particles of impure matter, like goat's droppings and cow dung, from touching his jallabeyya, since he would otherwise be obliged to change his clothes before going to the mosque again. This meant that he had to walk with extreme care in those liberally manured fields, with his hem plucked high above his ankles, very much in the manner that women hitch up their saris during the monsoons in Calcutta.

Before we had gone very far we came upon some of his relatives, working in a vegetable patch. They invited us to sit with them and began to ask me questions about the soil and the crops in India. Ustaz Mustafa soon grew impatient with this and led me away.

'They are fellaheen,' he said apologetically. 'They don't have much interest in religion or anything important.'

'I am just like that myself,' I said quickly.

'Really?' said Ustaz Mustafa, aghast. We walked in silence for a while, and then he said: 'I am giving up hope that you will become a Muslim.' Then an idea occurred to him and he turned to face me. 'Tell me,' he said, 'would your father be upset if you were to change your religion?'

'Maybe,' I said.

He relapsed into thoughtful silence for a few minutes. 'Has your father read the holy books of Islam?' he asked, eagerly.

'I don't know,' I answered.

'He must read them,' said Ustaz Mustafa. 'If he did he would surely convert himself.'

'I don't know,' I said. 'He is accustomed to his own ways.'

He mulled the issue over in his mind, and when we turned back towards Lataifa he said: 'Well, it would not be right for you to upset your father. That is true.'

After that the heart went out of his efforts to convert me: he had a son himself and it went against his deepest instincts to urge a man to turn against his father. And so, as the rival moralities of religion and kinship gradually played themselves to a standstill within him, Ustaz Mustafa and I came to an understanding.

A connection was already beginning to form in my mind now, as I turned towards Shaikh Musa's wife. 'Is Ustaz Mustafa really your uncle?' I asked her, uncertain of whether she was using the word in a specific or general sense. 'Your father's real brother, your 'amm shagîg?'

She was too shy to address me directly, at least in Ahmed's presence, so he spoke for her. 'Ustaz Mustafa is her real uncle,' he said. 'Her father and he were carried in the same belly. They still live in the same house.'

'But then Jabir must be her cousin,' I said in astonishment. 'They must have grown up in the same house.'

'Yes,' said Ahmed, 'she is Jabir's bint 'amm, his father's brother's daughter.'

He could have added: 'If Jabir were older he could have married her himself.' Certainly Jabir's parents and relatives would probably have wished for nothing better, since a marriage between first cousins, the children of brothers, was traditionally regarded as an ideal sort of union—a strengthening of an already existing bond.

'So she is of Abu-'Ali's lineage then?' I asked Ahmed.

'Yes,' said Ahmed, 'Abu-'Ali is her father's first cousin. His half-sister is her grandmother as well as Jabir's. She still lives in their house: you've met her.'

And so I had, a portly matriarch dressed in black, with fine features and delicate papery skin: she bore not the remotest resemblance to Abu-'Ali. I remembered her because of the posture of command she had assumed, perfectly naturally, with one knee flat on the floor and the other drawn up to support her arm and clenched fist. A glance from her had been enough to keep even Jabir quiet.

'Yes,' said Ahmed, 'Abu-'Ali's father was her great-grandfather's brother. And of course, his father, Abu-'Ali's grandfather, was my great-great-grandfather's brother.'

By this time I had lost my way in this labyrinth of relationships. It was only much later, when Shaikh Musa helped me draw up a complete genealogy of hamlet of Lataifa (all of whose inhabitants belonged ultimately to a single family called Laṭīf) that I finally began to see why he was always so careful never to voice a word of criticism about Abu-'Ali: his wife, Sakkina, was Abu-'Ali's great-grand-niece. The lines of the genealogy led inexorably to the conclusion that Abu-'Ali had played a crucial part in arranging the marriage.

It became clear to me then that there were complexities in Shaikh Musa's relationship with Abu-'Ali that I did not understand, and probably never would; that it would be deeply embarrassing for him if I were to ask him to help me find some other house, or family, to live in.

I realized then that my deliverance from Abu-'Ali would not come as easily as the dreams that took me to Cairo.

5

FOR BEN YIJU the centre of Cairo would have lain in a modest building near the eastern walls of the fortress of Babylon: the Synagogue of Ben Ezra, also known as the 'Synagogue of the Palestinians'. The building was destined to last until a good seven hundred years after Ben Yiju's lifetime; it was still standing late into the nineteenth century. In 1884 it was described, by a British historian and archæologist, A. J. Butler, as a small and somewhat simplified version of a Coptic basilica. By then most of its woodwork was gone and in 'point of detail there is not much remaining...'

When Ben Yiju first saw it, the building probably had a faint whiff of novelty about it, having been completely rebuilt only a hundred years or so earlier, in about 1025. It is known to have had two entrances then: one for the men, the main gateway, and a 'secret door' leading to a wooden platform inside the building, the women's gallery. The main chamber of the synagogue had a gabled ceiling and glass windows, and it was decorated with woodwork of very fine quality: some of it has survived and can still be seen in the Louvre, and in museums in Cairo and Jerusalem.

As far as Ben Yiju was concerned, his membership of this synagogue was probably more a matter of birth than personal preference. His origins lay in a region that was known as Ifrîqiya in the Arabic-speaking world of the Middle Ages—an area centred around what is now Tunisia. The region had fared badly in the eleventh century and over a period of several decades, since well before Ben Yiju's lifetime, its merchants and traders had been moving eastwards, towards Egypt. Jews figured prominently among these migrants and those amongst them who moved to Masr generally chose to join the 'Palestinian' congregation in Babylon. Ben Yiju was thus following a well-marked trail.

For the Synagogue of Ben Ezra the influx of migrants from Ifriqiya was to prove providential: the newcomers proved to be the most industrious members of the community and they soon assumed its leadership, setting the pattern for the others in matters of language and culture, as well as trade and commerce. The North Africans appear to have had a particular affinity for the flourishing trade between the Mediterranean and the Indian Ocean and over a period of several centuries the Jewish traders of Fustat counted as an integral part of the richly diverse body of merchants who were involved in the conduct of business in Asian waters. Carried along by the movements of that cycle of trade many of them travelled regularly between three continents—men whose surnames often read like the chapter headings of an epic, linked them to sleepy oases and dusty Saharan market towns, places like El Faiyum and Tlemcen.

Thus it was no ordinary congregation that Ben Yiju joined in Masr: it consisted of a group of people whose travels and breadth of experience and education seem astonishing even today, on a planet thought to be newly-shrunken. Yet, unlike others of that time who have left their mark on history, the members of this community were not born to privilege and entitlement; they were neither aristocrats nor soldiers nor professional scholastics. The vast majority of them were traders, and while some of them were wealthy and successful, they were not, by any means, amongst the most powerful merchants of their time—most of them were small traders running small family businesses. Yet, despite their generally modest circumstances, a majority of the men were endowed with a respectable level of education, and some were among the most learned scholars of their time. Their doctors, for example, studied Hippocrates and Galen in Arabic translation, as well as the medical writings of Arab physicians and scholars, such as Ibn Rushd (Averroes) and al-Râzî. Indeed, one member of the Synagogue's congregation is reckoned to have been one of the finest minds of the Middle Ages: the great doctor, scholar and philosopher Mûsa ibn Maimûn, known as Maimonides. Like so many others in his community, he too had close familial links with the India Trade.

The greatest achievement of the Ben Ezra congregation, however, was the product of largely fortuitous circumstances. The Synagogue's members followed a custom, widespread at the time, of depositing their writings in a special chamber in the synagogue so that they could be disposed of with special rites later. This practice, which is still observed among certain Jewish groups today, was intended to prevent the accidental desecration of any written form of God's name. Since most writings in that epoch included at least one sacred invocation in the course of the text, the custom effectively ensured that written documents of every kind were deposited within the Synagogue. The chambers in which the documents were kept were known by the term

'Geniza', a word that is thought to have come into Hebrew from a Persian root, ganj, meaning 'storehouse'—a common element in place-names in India and Iran, particularly beloved of the British who sprinkled it liberally across their Indian settlements, in odd Anglicized forms like 'Ballygunge' and 'Daltongunj'.

Every synagogue in the Middle East once had a Geniza and in accordance with custom, their contents were regularly emptied and buried. The Geniza of the Synagogue of Ben Ezra was added when the synagogue was rebuilt in 1025AD, but for some reason—possibly reverence for the past, possibly mere oversight—it was never cleared out. For more than eight centuries papers continued to accumulate inside the Geniza. At the peak of the community's prosperity, during the first two and a half centuries after the rebuilding of the Synagogue in 1025, great quantities of manuscripts poured in. Then, towards the middle of the thirteenth century, the flow dried to a trickle, and only swelled again some three hundred years later, when the Spanish Inquisition sent yet another wave of Jewish immigrants flooding in to Egypt. Papers (and later, books) continued to accumulate intermittently in the Geniza until the nineteenth century, by which time Fustat had become a poor neglected backwater in Cairo's rapidly expanding archipelago. The document that is thought to be the last to be deposited in the Geniza bears the date 1875: it was a divorce settlement written in Bombay.

For centuries the Synagogue of the Palestinians lay forgotten within the half-abandoned precincts of the ancient fortress of Babylon. In about 1890, the eleventh-century building, the structure that Ben Yiju saw, was finally torn down and a new one was erected in its place: it still stands on the site today.

Until recently the site of the Synagogue of Ben Ezra lay at one end of a plateau of rubble; an expanse of shattered brick and stone, that looked as though it had been flattened by a gigantic hammer. The Synagogue itself, an undistinguished, rectangular building, seemed just barely to have survived: much of its masonry had crumbled, and the shutters had fallen away from many of its windows. Its most striking feature was a pair of wrought-iron gates; although much discoloured and corroded, they were still graceful, their sinuous forms exuberantly Art Deco: they looked as though someone had ordered them from Paris in a flush of enthusiasm after a summer holiday. Above the narrow gateway, held in place by a length of iron tubing and a few heavy stones, was a Star of David, a little askew and festooned with cobwebs.

Today the building is once again rejuvenated, its exterior scrubbed and well-tended. Prefabricated huts have sprouted in the rubble outside, where young engineers stand behind drawing-boards, their toes tapping gently to the beat of muted rock music: a team of Canadian experts and restorers has arrived, Mountie-like, to rescue the Synagogue from the assaults of Time.

A few men wait for tourists at the entrance to the Synagogue, standing behind desks spread with beads, necklaces, bronze scarabs and busts of Nefertiti. One of them has been there for years, a plump, smiling man, dressed in a shirt and trousers. His trinkets and souvenirs do not seem to change much from year to year—in fact he never seems to do much business at all—but he is always full of smiles, good-natured, and helpful. He explains that 'Amm Shahata, the caretaker, is inside, he can take visitors in and explain everything—he is Jewish, yahûdi, he knows all about the Synagogue.

In a while 'Amm Shahata appears, a sprightly old man, very thin and a little stooped. He too is dressed in a shirt and trousers, and his skull-cap is very much like any Egyptian Muslim's. The two men exchange some companionable banter; his Arabic is indistinguishable from theirs, the staccato speech of working-class Cairo. He tells you his name: 'Nathan in Hebrew and Shahata in Arabic.' Close up he looks unexpectedly old, his teeth are gone and veins stand out on his forehead.

'Amm Shahata soon lets it be known that he is a busy man: he has no time to waste; he ushers you briskly through the gateway and leads you into the main chamber of the Synagogue. Prisms of light shine through coloured windows; you are in a room with a very high ceiling, but otherwise of modest, schoolroom size. In the centre is a raised, octagonal altar, with benches arranged in rows on either side. The room has two levels. At the upper level is the women's gallery, which runs around three sides of the room. At the far end of the gallery, on the left, is a small hole, high up in the wall; it opens into an empty chamber adjoining the back wall. 'Amm Shahata points at the opening; that is the Geniza, he tells you, where a lot of papers were found, years and years ago.

You wish it were indeed the old Geniza, but it cannot be. It is no higher than a bare six feet or so while the Geniza of the old Synagogue is known to have been at least as tall as the rest of the building, some two and a half storeys high. The old Geniza was probably left standing for a while, after the rest of the structure was torn down, but it must have perished later.

Of course, you have no cause to be disappointed. The Synagogue's location has not altered, whatever the changes in its outer shell. The fact is that you are standing upon the very site which held the greatest single collection of medieval documents ever discovered.

It was here, in this forlorn corner of Masr, that the memories of Abraham Ben Yiju and his slave lay preserved for more than seven hundred years.

6

ONCE, ON A very hot afternoon, when the sweat was dribbling off my face on to my notebooks, I gave up trying to work, and sat in my room with the door open, hoping to trap a breath of fresh air. It was very still that day, with the moisture from the freshly-watered cotton fields and rice paddies hanging heavy in the air. At intervals, as though frightened by the stillness, the ducks and chickens with whom I shared the roof would burst into an uproar, erupt out of their coops and flap around the roof in a gale of frenzied squawks, undaunted by the flat, white heat of the afternoon.

As I sat watching, a pair of ducks began to race around and around the roof, one in pursuit of the other. They were of a species I had never seen before I came to Egypt: squat, ugly creatures, almost suicidally self-absorbed, with large red warts on their necks and mangy black and white bodies. The pursuer was the bigger of the two, and it soon caught up with the other and pinned it to the floor with its beak. Then, after it had hoisted itself on top, it raised one leg and suddenly its penis appeared, a bright, wet pink, about as long as a thumbnail. It flapped its tailfeathers for a moment, pressing against its mate, and then tumbled off, a look of bafflement on its face. I watched spellbound: I had had no conception that ducks had penises and vaginas.

I happened to look up then and I saw Jabir, standing silently in the stairway, watching me.

He began to laugh.

'You were watching like it was a film, ya Amitab,' he said, laughing. 'Haven't you seen ducks do that before?'

'No,' I said.

His laughter was infectious; I found myself laughing with him.

He came into the room and seated himself on the chair, taking care to keep his clean jallabeyya from touching the floor.

'So tell me then,' he said, throwing me a glance of interested inquiry. 'What do you know on the subject of...?'

He used a word I had not heard before. I must have looked puzzled, for he gave an incredulous gasp and said: 'You mean you've never heard of...?'

It was the same word again.

I shook my head and he sank back in the chair, knocking his head with his fist, nearly dislodging his white skull-cap.

'Ya Amitab,' he said in mock despair. 'What are you going to do in life if you don't know about that?'

'About what?' I said.

This only made him laugh. 'If you don't know you don't know,' he muttered mysteriously.

'Don't know about what?' I said, in exasperation.

'It's not important,' he said, grinning, elliptical. 'It's good to put a distance between your thoughts and things like that. But tell me this—of course you have circumcision where you come from, just like we do? Isn't that so, mush kida?'

I had long been dreading this line of questioning, knowing exactly where it would lead.

'Some people do,' I said. 'And some people don't.'

'You mean,' he said in rising disbelief, 'there are people in your country who are not circumcised?'

In Arabic the word 'circumcise' derives from a root that means 'to purify': to say of someone that they are 'uncircumcised' is more or less to call them impure.

'Yes,' I answered, 'yes, many people in my country are "impure".' I had no alternative; I was trapped by language.

'But not you…' He could not bring himself to finish the sentence.

'Yes,' I said. My face was hot with embarrassment and my throat had gone dry: 'Yes, me too.'

He gasped and his incredulous eyes skimmed over the front of my trousers. For a moment he stared in disbelieving curiosity, and then, with an effort, he said: 'And when you go to the barber to have your hair cut, do you not shave your armpits like we do?'

'No,' I said.

He leant forward, frowning intently. 'So tell me then,' he said, pointing a finger at my crotch. 'Don't you shave there either?'

'No,' I said.

'But then,' he cried, 'doesn't the hair grow longer and longer until…'

Inadvertently his eyes dropped and he stole a quick look at my ankles. I am convinced, to this day, that he fully expected to see the ends of two long, curly braids peeping out from the ends of my trousers.

That evening, towards sunset, I went for a walk in the fields. A fair distance from the hamlet I came upon Jabir and some other boys of his age, sitting beside a small canal. They had their textbooks with them and they were taking advantage of the comparative quiet of the fields to catch up with their schoolwork. I stopped dead when I saw Jabir; I was not sure whether we were still on speaking terms. But to my relief he waved cheerfully when he saw me coming, and then he and his friends jumped to their feet and fell in beside me.

'You should go on with your studies,' I said. 'There's still plenty of light.'

'We should be returning now,' Jabir said, 'it will soon be time for the evening prayers. Look—the moon is already up.'

I looked up and saw a full moon, brilliant against the fading purple of the evening sky. It was very quiet, except for the creak of distant water-wheels; in Lataifa, far away, the first lamps were beginning to shine.

Jabir had his arms around the shoulders of the other boys. 'Do you want to hear something?' he said. He was whispering but I could hear him clearly in the sunset hush.

'I was talking to him this afternoon,' he said, gesturing at me with his chin. 'And do you know, he doesn't know what sex is?'

I had checked in the dictionary as soon as he'd left: he was using the same word he'd used that afternoon.

'What's this you're saying, ya Jabir?' one of the boys exclaimed. 'He doesn't know what sex is?'

'What am I telling you?' Jabir retorted. 'He doesn't know. I asked him.'

'And he looks so grown up and all.'

'But he doesn't know a thing,' said Jabir. 'Not religion, not politics, not sex, just like a child.'

There was an awed silence. 'Do you think he doesn't know about "beating the ten" either?' one of the boys whispered. I was not familiar with this expression at the time, but the gesture of the fist that accompanied it gave me a fair idea of its meaning.

'No,' said Jabir, 'he's like a child, I told you. That's why he's always asking questions.'

'Shouldn't we tell him?' one of the boys said. 'How's he going to grow up if he doesn't beat the ten?'

'It's no use,' said Jabir. 'He won't understand; he doesn't know a thing. Look, I'll show you.'

He detached himself from the others and called out to me: 'Ya Amitab—stop, wait a minute.'

Taking hold of my elbow he led me to the edge of the canal. 'Look at that,' he said, pointing at the reflection of the full moon on the water. 'What is it? Do you know?'

'Of course I know,' I scoffed. 'It's Ahmed, Shaikh Musa's son, shining his torch on the water.'

There was a hushed silence and Jabir turned to cast the others a triumphant look while I walked on quickly.

'No, ya Amitab,' one of the boys said, running after me, his voice hoarse with concern. 'That's not so. It's not Ahmed shining his torch in the water—that's a reflection of the full moon.'

'No,' I said. 'You're absolutely wrong. Ahmed told me he would be going out for a walk today with his torch.'

'But if it's Ahmed how is it that we didn't see him?'

'We didn't see him because he was a long way off. His torch is very powerful. It works on four batteries. He's just bought new batteries—yesterday in Damanhour.'

And thus we argued, back and forth, and by the time we reached Lataifa I had nearly won the argument.

7

FOR A LONG time afterwards, I remained a child in Jabir's eyes.

One evening, shortly after the start of Ramadan (which stretched over July and August that year), Jabir took me to a mowlid, a fair in honour of a saint's birthday, in a village that lay across the fields. Several other boys from Lataifa went with us, among them Jabir's younger brother, Mohammad, and a nephew of Shaikh Musa's, a shy, quiet boy of fifteen, called Mabrouk.

As we walked across the fields towards the distant lights of the mowlid, Jabir and the other boys told me about the legend of Sidi 'Abbas of Nakhlatain, in whose honour the mowlid was being celebrated.

Sidi 'Abbas had lived in Nakhlatain long, long ago, long before anyone could remember, and he had been famous throughout the region for his godliness and piety: people had said of him that he was a 'good man', gifted with 'baraka', the power of conferring blessings. Such was his fame that a large crowd gathered in his village when he died, and so many people were witness to the miraculous events that graced his funeral. Trying to lift the Sidi's bier, the men of the village found, to their amazement, that they couldn't move it at all; dozens of them tried, only to find that they could not so much as budge it. It was only when the Sidi's son lent a hand that the body began to move, but even then, it was not he who moved the body: the Sidi had moved of his own volition.

The Sidi's body had led the wonderstruck people of the village into a mosque, and there the Sidi had communicated with them, telling them to build him a domed tomb, a maqâm: they were to celebrate his mowlid there every year. The people of the village had done as he had said, and in the following years the Sidi demonstrated his power to them time and time again, through miracles and acts of grace. Once, for instance, some thieves who were escaping with a herd of stolen water-buffalo were frozen to the ground, buffaloes and all, when they drew abreast of the Sidi's tomb. Such was the Sidi's power that anything left touching his tomb was safe: farmers who were late going home in the evening would even leave such valuable things as their wooden ploughs leaning against its walls, knowing that they would not be touched. Once, someone left a plough with leather thongs there, propped up against the tomb. After a while a mouse came along and, since mice like to nibble at leather, it had bitten into the plough's thongs. But no sooner had its teeth touched the plough than it was frozen to the ground; that was how it was found next morning, with its teeth stuck in the thongs. Even animals were not exempt from the rules of sanctuary that surrounded the Sidi's tomb.

The tomb was visible from a long way off, across the fields: a simple, rectangular structure with a low dome and a large open space in front which served as a public space—a common threshing-floor, as well as the site of the village's weekly market. Now the tomb was festooned with dozens of small bulbs, its freshly whitewashed walls dotted with puddles of coloured light. The square in front was crowded with people, some thronging into the tomb, and others circulating amongst the fairground stalls that had been erected all around it.

A stall-owner called out to us as we walked into the square. 'Come on,' he said, 'let's see what you young fellows can do.'

There were several airguns balanced on his counter, pointing at a board with dangling balloons and candles. Smiling encouragement, he thrust a couple of guns into our hands. I was stooping to take aim when I heard Jabir's voice behind me:

'From India…'

I looked over my shoulder and quickly turned back again. A large crowd had gathered around me; much larger than the crowds in any of the other stalls. 'Doesn't know anything,' I heard Jabir say, 'Nothing at all…' I squeezed the trigger, trying to keep my sights steady on a large balloon.

'You missed,' said Jabir.

Ignoring my mumbled retort, he turned back to his audience. 'Didn't I tell you?' he whispered. 'Doesn't know a thing.'

I tried to fix the balloon in my sights again, while people clustered eagerly around Jabir. 'Doesn't pray, doesn't even know Our Lord…'

'What're you saying? Doesn't know Our Lord!'

I squeezed the trigger, and once again the pellet thudded into the board, wide of the balloon.

'Doesn't know the Lord! Oh the Saviour!'

I shuffled off quickly to the next stall where a boy was selling pink, fluffy candy. Jabir's voice followed me: 'Reads books and asks questions all day long; doesn't have any work to do…'

'Can we talk to him?' somebody asked.

'No,' Jabir said magisterially. 'He won't understand a word you say. Only we in Lataifa know how to talk to him.'

I began to push my way quickly through the crowd, towards the other end of the square: I was hoping to put a distance between myself and Jabir, but he was not to be shaken off and followed hard on my heels. But then, providentially, I earned a brief respite; he and his cousins spotted a row of swings on the edge of the square and went running off to join the queue.

By the time I worked my way through the crowd their turns had come and they were heaving themselves back and forth, their jallabeyyas ballooning out around them, each trying to outdo the other. The crowd began to cheer them on and one of the boys swung high enough to go all the way around the bar in a complete circle. Jabir attempted a couple of mighty heaves himself, to no effect, so he jumped off, shrugging dismissively. 'I wasn't trying,' he said, dusting his hands. 'I can do it when I try.'

Then he marched us off across the square again, towards the Sidi's tomb. 'We should see the zikr,' he said sternly to his cousins. 'That's the most important part of the mowlid.'

A group of about thirty men, of all ages, had gathered in front of the tomb. Standing in rows, with their feet apart, they were jerking their heads and their torsos from side to side while a man dressed in a white turban chanted into a microphone. They swung their bodies in time with the rhythm, only their heads and their upper bodies moving, their feet perfectly still.

'They are Sûfis,' Jabir said for my benefit. 'They are invoking God by chanting his name.'

Some of the men had shut their eyes, and the others looked rapt, mesmerized by the rhythm and the movement. As the singer increased the tempo, their heads began to move faster, keeping time, their eyes becoming increasingly glazed, unseeing.

Jabir and his cousins were soon bored by the zikr. 'Makes me dizzy,' one of them said, and we went off to look at the stalls again.

It was not long before Jabir had a new audience.

'Doesn't know Our Lord, doesn't know anything…if you ask him how water-wheels are made, he'll say: "They have babies".'

'Oh the black day!'

'No!'

'Go on, ask him.'

'Do water-wheels have babies, ya doktór?' one of the boys said.

'No,' I said. 'They lay eggs.'

'Did you hear that? He thinks water-wheels lay eggs.'

I began to yearn for the solitude of my room, and to my relief, I did not have to wait long before the boys decided to head back across the cotton fields.

Early next morning, Jabir burst in, his face flushed with excitement. 'Do you know what happened last night?' he said, shaking me out of bed. 'There was a murder—a man was murdered at the mowlid.'

'What happened?' I said confusedly.

It had happened near the swings, Jabir said, exactly where we had been last night. The murdered man had been sitting on a swing when someone had come along and asked him to get off. He was pushed when he refused, and had fallen off and died, hitting his head on a rock.

And now, Jabir said, drawing himself up to his full height, there would be a blood feud. That was the law of the Arabs: 'Me and my brother against my cousin; me and my cousin against the stranger.' This was a serious matter: if a man killed someone, then he and all his male kin on the paternal side could be killed in revenge by the dead man's family. They would have to go and hide with their maternal relatives until their uncles and the shaikhs of the land could talk to the dead man's family and persuade them to come to a council of reconciliation. Then, when the grief of the dead man's family had eased a little, an amnesty would be declared. The two lineages would meet in some safe central place, and in the presence of their elders they would negotiate a blood-money payment. That was thâr, the law of feud; damm, the law of blood; the ancient, immutable law of the Arabs.

'All that for pushing a man off a swing?' I asked, bleary-eyed.

Jabir paused to think. 'Well, maybe a little one,' he said wistfully. 'Just a small feud.'

'Who was the man who was killed?'

'His name was Fathy,' said Jabir, 'but people called him "the Sparrow". He was from the village down the road: Nashawy. Now there'll be a feud there.'

I was somehow very doubtful, but for all the attention Jabir paid me, I could have been a six-year-old child.

8

IT WAS MABROUK, Shaikh Musa's nephew, who was responsible for improving my standing in Jabir's eyes.

That year Mabrouk's father had done exceptionally well from his vegetable plot. He'd taken a risk the autumn before by planting a lot of carrots after the cotton harvest. Everyone had tried to dissuade him—his wife, his brothers (including Shaikh Musa) and most of his cousins and relatives. The carrots would have to be harvested all at the same time, they had said, and what if the prices in the market were low that week? He would end up selling a whole truckload of carrots at a loss; it was better to plant many different kinds of vegetables, less of a risk.

Mabrouk's father had not paid any attention. He was an obstinate sort of man, and their arguments had only served to settle his resolve. As it turned out, he had been lucky. The price of carrots happened to be exceptionally high at the time of his harvest, and he made an unexpectedly large profit.

A few weeks later, he put all his savings together, and he and two of his brothers hired a truck and went off to Damanhour. When the truck returned, several hours later, the three brothers —all men of ample girth—were sitting in front, squeezed in beside the driver. In the back was a mysterious object, about as big as a calf but of a different shape, wrapped in several sheets of tarpaulin. The truck went quietly around to Mabrouk's house, and the object was unloaded and carried in through a back entrance, still wrapped in its tarpaulin sheets.

I knew nothing of this until Mabrouk burst into my room that afternoon: I heard the sound of feet flying up the stairs, and then Mabrouk threw the door open and caught hold of my arm.

'Come with me, ya doktór,' he cried. 'You have to come with me right now, to our house. My father and my family want you.' He was in a state of such feverish excitement that he could not bring himself to wait until I closed my notebook; he virtually dragged me out of the room right then, never letting go of my elbow.

Abu-'Ali and his family were astonished to see Mabrouk racing through their house, for he had always had a reputation for being unusually shy. Jabir told me once that despite being the tallest and fastest amongst the boys of their age, Mabrouk wasn't allowed to play in the forward line of their soccer team: the sight of an open goal was sometimes enough to bring on one of his attacks of shyness.

But now, Mabrouk was transformed; as we hurried through the lanes he talked volubly about how his father and his uncles had hired a truck and gone to Damanhour. But when I asked what exactly they had bought, he shook his head and smiled enigmatically. 'Wait, wait,' he said, 'you will see.'

By the time we got there, a crowd had collected in Mabrouk's lane, and his house was in an uproar. His father had been waiting for me, and after a hurried exchange of greetings, he spirited me past the crowd in his guest-room and led me quickly to a walled courtyard at the back, next to the pen where the livestock was kept—the most secret, secluded part of the house, the zarîba. Their acquisition was standing in the middle of the courtyard, like a newborn calf, with an old shoe hanging around it to fend off the Evil Eye.

It was a brand-new diesel water-pump, the first of its kind to come to Lataifa. There were several such pumps in the surrounding villages: they were known generically as 'al-makana al-Hindi', the Indian machine, for they were all manufactured in India.

Mabrouk, his father, his mother and several cousins and uncles, were standing around me now, in a circle, looking from me to the machine, bright-eyed and expectant.

'Makana hindi!' I said to Mabrouk's father, with a show of enthusiasm. 'Congratulations—you've bought an "Indian machine"!'

Mabrouk's father's eyes went misty with pride as he gazed upon the machine. 'Yes,' he sighed. 'Yes, that's why we asked you to come. You must take a look at it and tell us what you think.'

'Me?' I said. I was aghast; I knew nothing at all about water-pumps; indeed, I could not recall ever having noticed one before coming to Lataifa.

'Yes!' Mabrouk's father clapped me on the back. 'It's from your country, isn't it? I told the dealer in Damanhour, I said, "Make sure you give me one that works well, we have an Indian living in our hamlet and he'll be able to tell whether we've got a good one or not."'

I hesitated, mumbling a few words of protest, but he nudged me eagerly forward. A quick look at the anxious, watchful faces around me told me that escape was impossible: I would have to pronounce an opinion, whether I liked it or not.

A hush fell upon the courtyard as I walked up to the machine; a dozen heads craned forward, watching my every move. I went up to the machine's spout, stooped beside it and peered knowledgeably into its inky interior, shutting one eye. Standing up again, I walked around the pump amidst a deathly silence, nodding to myself, occasionally tapping parts of it with my knuckles. Then, placing both hands on the diesel motor, I fell to my knees and shut my eyes. When I looked up again Mabrouk's father was standing above me, anxiously awaiting the outcome of my silent communion with this product of my native soil.

Reaching for his hand I gave it a vigorous shake. 'It's a very good makana Hindi,' I said, patting the pump's diesel tank. 'Excellent! 'Azeem! It's an excellent machine.'

At once a joyful hubbub broke out in the courtyard. Mabrouk's father pumped my hand and slapped me on the back. 'Tea,' he called out to his wife. 'Get the doktór al-Hindi some tea.'

Next day Jabir came to visit me in my room, late in the evening. He seemed somehow subdued, much quieter and less cocky than usual.

'I was talking to Mabrouk,' he said, 'I heard he took you to his house to see their new "Indian machine".'

I shrugged nonchalantly. 'Yes,' I said. 'He did.'

'And what was your opinion?' he asked.

'They've bought a good machine,' I said. 'A very good one.'

Jabir sank into silence, nodding thoughtfully. Later, when he rose to leave, he stopped at the door and declared: 'My father and my uncles are thinking of buying an Indian machine too, insha'allah.'

'Good,' I said.

'I hope you'll come with us,' he said.

'Where?'

'When we go to Damanhour to buy it,' he said, shyly. 'We would profit from your opinion.'

I stayed up a long time that night, marvelling at the respect the water-pump had earned me; I tried to imagine where I would have stood in Jabir's eyes if mine had been a country that exported machines that were even bigger, better and more impressive—cars and tractors perhaps, not to speak of ships and planes and tanks. I began to wonder how Lataifa would have looked if I had had the privilege of floating through it, protected by the delegated power of technology, of looking out untroubled through a sheet of clear glass.

9

SOON THE MONTH of Ramadan arrived and I began to think of taking a holiday. First I would go to Alexandria, I decided, to talk to Doctor Issa, and to see whether I could make arrangements for moving out of Abu-'Ali's house. After that I would go to Cairo: I had spent one night there when I first arrived, but I had seen nothing other than the airport, and the station. Now at last, the time had come to pay the city a proper visit.

As the days passed the thought of my trip became ever more exciting. We were then well into Ramadan, and I was one of the handful of people in the hamlet who were not fasting. I had wanted to join in the fast, but everyone insisted, 'No, you can't fast, you're not Muslim—only Muslims fast at Ramadan.' And so, being reminded of my exclusion every day by the drawn, thirsty faces around me, the thought of Cairo and Alexandria, and the proximity of others among the excluded, grew ever more attractive.

From the very first day of the lunar month the normal routines of the village had undergone a complete change: it was as though a segment of time had been picked from the calendar and turned inside out. Early in the morning, a good while before sunrise, a few young men would go from house to house waking everyone for the suḥûr, the early morning meal. After that, as the day progressed, a charged lassitude would descend upon Lataifa. To ease the rigours of the fast people would try to finish all their most pressing bits of work early in the morning, while the sun was still low in the sky; it was impossible to do anything strenuous on an empty stomach and parched throat once the full heat of the day had set in. By noon the lanes of the hamlet would be still, deserted. The women would be in their kitchens and oven-rooms, getting their meals ready for the breaking of the fast at sunset. The men would sit in the shade of trees, or in their doorways, fanning themselves. Their mouths and lips would sometimes acquire thin white crusts, and often, as the hours wore on, their tempers would grow brittle.

I often wondered whether there were any people in the village who were occasionally delinquent in their observance of the fast. It was true that the most vulnerable people—pregnant women, young children, the sick, the elderly, and so on—were exempted by religious law, but even for those of sound body the fast must have been very hard: those were long, fiercely hot summer days, and it must have been difficult indeed to last through them without food, water or tobacco. Yet I never once saw a single person in Lataifa breaking the fast, in any way: there were occasional rumours that certain people in such and such village had been seen eating or drinking, but even those were very rare.

In every house as the sun sank slowly towards the horizon, the women would lay out their trays and serve the food they had cooked during the day. Their families would gather around, ravenous now, with cool, tall glasses of water resting in front of them. They would sit watching the lengthening shadows, tense and still, listening to their radios, waiting for the shaikhs of the mosque of al-Azhar in Cairo to announce the legal moment of sunset. It was not enough to see the sun going down with one's eyes; the breaking of the fast was the beginning of a meal of communion that embraced millions of people and the moment had to be celebrated publicly and in unison.

When the meal was finished and the trays had been cleared away, the men would wash and change and make their way to the mosque, talking, laughing, replete with a sense of well-being which the day's denials had made multiply sweet. I would go up to my room alone and listen to the call of the muezzin and try to think of how it must feel to know that on that very day, as the sun travelled around the earth, millions and millions of people in every corner of the globe had turned to face the same point, and said exactly the same words of prayer, with exactly the same prostrations as oneself. A phenomenon on that scale was beyond my imagining, but the exercise helped me understand why so many people in the hamlet had told me not to fast: to belong to that immense community was a privilege which they had to re-earn every year, and the effort made them doubly conscious of the value of its boundaries.

In the evenings, after the prayers, the hamlet would be full of life and laughter. Where at other times of the year the lanes and paths were generally empty by eight o' clock, they were now full of bustle and activity: children going from house to house, chanting and demanding gifts, and people visiting their families and staying up late, gossiping and joking with their friends.

The night before I left for my trip to Cairo and Alexandria, I went to see Shaikh Musa to say goodbye. He and his family were resting after breaking the day's fast. They had eaten well and Shaikh Musa had just returned from the mosque. He was sitting on a mat in his bedroom, puffing on his shusha, a home-made hookah, making up for all the tobacco he had had to deny himself during the day.

He was in high spirits. 'Welcome, ya Amitab,' he said. 'How are you, come and sit here, beside me.'

As soon as I'd sat down he pointed at a young man sitting across the room and said: 'Do you know who that is?'

The room was lit only by the glow of a single oil lamp, but I recognized the young man he had pointed to the moment I saw him. It was his younger son Hasan. He looked very much like the photograph Shaikh Musa carried in his wallet: robust, with clean, chiselled features, and a pleasant, rather shy smile. He lifted his right hand to his heart to welcome me to his house, and we shook hands and exchanged the customary greetings.

'You have brought blessings.'

'God bless you.'

'You have brought light to our house.'

'The light is yours.'

His face was sunburnt, ruddy, and he was wearing the khaki fatigues of the Egyptian army.

'He's on leave,' Shaikh Musa said. 'The army let him go for a few days so he could visit his family.'

Just then Sakkina appeared in the doorway and handed Hasan a tray with three glasses of tea on it. He took it from her without a word and she disappeared back into the kitchen. Neither she nor Hasan spoke to each other, but it struck me suddenly that they were probably of exactly the same age: as children they would have worked in the same groups in the cotton fields, picking weevils from the plants, and they would have played together in the hamlet's threshing-grounds in the evenings. I could not help wondering about the nuances of their present situation, about how they dealt with each other as stepmother and stepson.

'He got here this afternoon,' Shaikh Musa said. 'He's been travelling all morning.'

I asked Hasan where he had come from and he told me that he was posted in Mansourah, a small town a couple of hundred miles away, at the other end of the Delta. His voice sounded tired and when he had finished speaking he leant his head back against the wall.

'He's not well,' Shaikh Musa explained. 'He's got a pain in the head.'

I saw then that he had a bandage tied around his forehead. I had not noticed it before for it was largely hidden by his thick, dark hair.

'He comes home for a day and look what happens to him,' Shaikh Musa said in mock outrage. 'Shouldn't the government extend his leave, at least?'

In a short while other people began to arrive. Some were relatives who had heard that Hasan was back on leave, and some were friends of Shaikh Musa's from nearby villages. I soon realized that some of them were from Nashawy, and the moment there was a break in the conversation I asked if there was going to be a feud in their village. They looked at one another in puzzlement at first, and when I recounted the story that Jabir had told me they began to laugh.

The boy had imagined it, they said. There would be no feud, even though it was true that the man called the Sparrow had died. The police had made a report, and it had been settled between the two families. The Sparrow had been a poor man, none too sound in the head, with very few relatives in the area. The man who had knocked him over was from a big and powerful family. There was no question of a feud: the elders of the two families had sat down and decided on a token payment and that was that, khalas.

Shaikh Musa, listening intently, sighed and shook his head. 'Nashawy!' he said. 'There's always some trouble there.'

It was a big, bustling place, Nashawy, with almost fourteen hundred people, fully a thousand more than Lataifa! All those people living crowded together; no wonder they had trouble.

They began to talk about Nashawy, and listening to them I wondered why I had not visited the village yet. It was just a mile or so down the road, and I would often hear the drivers of the pick-up trucks that went past Lataifa shouting 'Nashawy? Nashawy?' In my first few weeks in the hamlet I had often thought of climbing on for the ride. But now I had heard the name so often that it had begun to sound like a challenge: it had become a place that I would have to prepare for, just as I was preparing myself for Cairo.

A little later, when I got up to leave, Shaikh Musa's guests invited me to visit Nashawy, but Shaikh Musa cut them short. 'He doesn't have time now,' he said. 'He's going to Cairo, to Masr.'

He and his two sons came to the door to say goodbye. Shaikh Musa stood in the middle, holding his two grandsons by the hand, his eldest son, Ahmed, on his right and Hasan, the younger, on his left. 'Come back soon, ya mister,' he said, 'and tell us about your trip. We want to hear about it, about Masr.'

'I'll tell you about it,' I said, 'as soon as I return.'

At the end of the lane, I looked back: Shaikh Musa was still there, the picture of happiness and fulfilment, surrounded by his sons and grandsons.

'Do you know what they say about Masr?' he shouted after me. 'They say she's the umm al-duniyâ, the "mother of the world".'

10

IN THE EIGHTEENTH century, a new breed of traveller began to flock into Cairo, Europeans with scholarly and antiquarian interests, for whom Masr was merely the picturesque but largely incidental location of an older, and far more important landscape. By this time Europe was far in advance of the rest of the world in armaments and industry, and on the points of those weapons the high age of imperialism was about to be ushered in. Masr had long since ceased to be the mistress of her own destiny; she had become a province of the Ottoman Empire, which was itself enfeebled now, allowed to keep its territories only by the consent of the Great Powers. The Indian Ocean trade, and the culture that supported it, had long since been destroyed by European navies. Transcontinental trade was no longer a shared enterprise; the merchant shipping of the high seas was now entirely controlled by the naval powers of Europe. It no longer fell to Masr to send her traders across the Indian Ocean; instead, the geographical position that had once brought her such great riches had now made her the object of the Great Powers' attentions, as a potential bridge to their territories in the Indian Ocean.

Over the same period that Egypt was gaining a new strategic importance within the disposition of European empires, she was also gradually evolving into a new continent of riches for the Western scholarly and artistic imagination. From the late seventeenth century onwards, Europe was swept by a fever of Egyptomania: sphinxes and pyramids began to appear in houses and gardens throughout the continent; several operas were written around themes from ancient Egypt; a succession of Popes became interested in the placing of Rome's obelisks, and none other than Sir Isaac Newton took it upon himself to prove that Osiris, Bacchus, Sesostris and Sisac were but different names for the same deity. Concurrent with this growing interest, the study of Egyptian antiquities passed from being an esoteric and quasi-mystical pursuit into a freshly-charted field of scholarly enterprise, and in the service of the new science several travellers undertook journeys of discovery into Egypt.

It was against this background that the first report of the Geniza was published in Europe. In 1752 or '53, a Jewish traveller, Simon Van Geldern, an ancestor of the German poet Heinrich Heine, visited the Synagogue of Ben Ezra, in Babylon. The visit appears to have been an unremarkable one: all that Van Geldern had to say of it was that he had 'looked around' the Geniza and paid five coins. Effectively, the event passed unnoticed. At that time European scholarly interest was focused on the Egypt of the ancients; the Synagogue of Ben Ezra was too much a part of Masr to merit attention.

By the end of the eighteenth century, Egypt had become the scholarly counterpart of those great landmasses that were then being claimed and explored by European settlers: unknown to herself, she was already well on her way to becoming a victim of the Enlightenment's conceptions of knowledge and discovery. In fact, the first detailed plan for the conquest of Egypt was conceived not by a soldier but by a philosopher, Karl Liebniz, as early as 1670. More than a hundred years later, when Napoleon conceived of his invasion of Egypt, it was partly on the model of a scientific expedition.

In the decades immediately after Napoleon's invasion of 1798, Egypt attracted the husbandry of the Western academy in a way that no other place ever had. Yet all through this period, despite the concentrated efforts being expended on the soil around it, the Geniza remained entirely unnoticed: it was then still a part of a living tradition, and the conquering scholars had little interest in the dishevelled and unglamorous inhabitants of contemporary Masr.

More than a hundred years passed after Simon Van Geldern's visit with no public notice being taken of the Geniza at the Synagogue of Ben Ezra. By the time the next reports were published, Masr had passed into the control of the British, and her position on the route to India had become her curse, the proximate cause of her annexation. The visit that first brought the Geniza to the attention of the scholarly world occurred in 1864, and then, soon enough, events began to unfold quietly around it, in a sly allegory on the intercourse between power and the writing of history.

In the summer of 1864, when the construction of the Suez

Canal was well under way and Egypt was being readied, once again, to become the stepping-stone to India, a scholar and collector of Judaic antiquities by the name of Jacob Saphir paid several visits to the Synagogue of Ben Ezra while passing through Egypt. The synagogue was still greatly venerated by the Jewish inhabitants of Cairo, and travellers were often directed to it as a site worthy of pilgrimage.

On his visits, Saphir had the Geniza pointed out to him from a distance and was told that it contained many worn and tattered old books. But when he asked to look into the chamber he met with a flat refusal. There was a snake curled up at the entrance, the officials of the synagogue told him, and it would be extremely dangerous to go in. Their refusal made Saphir all the more determined to investigate, and he returned to the Synagogue after obtaining permission to enter the chamber from the head of the Rabbinical court. The officials were not impressed, and they told him, laughing: 'Can a man risk his life for nothing? He won't even live out the year!' They relented only when Saphir assured them that he knew how to charm snakes, and promised them a reward.

As Saphir found it, the Geniza was full to a height of two and a half storeys; it was open to the sky on top, and strewn with rubble and debris within. He left after spending two exhausting days inside, without encountering 'any fiery serpents or scorpions', and taking only a 'few leaves from various old books and manuscripts'. Upon closer examination, none of those fragments proved to be of any value, but describing his visit in his memoirs, Saphir added the rider: 'But who knows what is still beneath?'

His account appeared in 1866, arousing interest within a small circle of scholars, and lending credence to rumours that a potential treasure trove of documents was waiting to be uncovered in Cairo.

The Synagogue of Ben Ezra was probably visited again, soon afterwards, by a man who eventually put together one of the largest collections of Hebrew manuscripts in the world. He was a Crimean Jew of the Karaite sect, Abraham Firkowitch, a collector renowned as much for his unscrupulousness as for his fine judgement. The collection he assembled over his lifetime is now in the State Public Library in St. Petersburg. The manuscripts were bought in two lots: Firkowitch sold the first one himself, and the second was acquired soon after his death in 1874. The second lot alone contains about fifteen times as many Biblical manuscripts as there are in the British Museum. The German scholar Paul Kahle, who devoted the better part of a lifetime to the study of Firkowitch's collection, estimated that in all the libraries of Europe, taken together, there were not even as many as a third of the number of Biblical manuscripts as there were in this one collection in St. Petersurg. It is known that many of these documents were from the Cairo Geniza, but as to which they were there is no way of knowing because Firkowitch never revealed his sources. He had obtained many of his documents by swindling synagogue officials in various parts of the Middle East, and it was his practice to conceal his collecting methods behind a veil of secrecy.

If there is an irony today in the thought that a Jewish collector, not so very long ago, would have seen reason to steal manuscripts from his fellow Jews in Palestine in order to take them to Russia, it is not one that would have been apparent to Firkowitch: he was merely practising on his co-religionists the methods that Western scholarship used, as a normal part of its functioning, throughout the colonized world.

Over the next few years more and more Geniza documents began to change hands. Already in the 1880s substantial quantities were being carried away to Palestine, Europe and the USA—by collectors who were often still unaware of the very existence of the Geniza. Towards the end of that decade, in 1888, a Jewish Briton, who was to play an important part in the dispersal of the Geniza, happened to spend Yom Kippur in the company of some of the prominent Jewish families of Cairo. His name was Elkan N. Adler, and upon his return to London he published an account of his visit in the *Jewish Chronicle*. He took issue there with those of his fellow British Jews who passed through Cairo and showed no interest in its Jewish community. For his own part he declared himself to be very well-satisfied with his experience. 'It is not often,' he wrote, 'that a European has the opportunity of joining the aborigines in celebrating their feasts.'

In the course of his visit Adler had developed an acquaintance with a family that held a position of enormous influence within the city's Jewish community; their name was Cattaoui and they were to play a critical part in the subsequent history of the Geniza. The Cattaouis are thought to have come to Egypt by way of Holland and like most of the leading Jewish families of Cairo in the late nineteenth century, they were Sephardic rather than 'Oriental' Jews. By this time the indigenous Jews of Cairo, those whose relationship with the Synagogue of Ben Ezra was most direct, were a small and impoverished minority within the community. The Cattaouis had themselves once lived in a Jewish enclave of Cairo, but they were one of the first families to come out of the ḥâra. They had gone on to establish a prosperous banking firm with offices in Cairo, Alexandria and Paris, and at the time of Adler's visit they were by far the most powerful family within the community.

The founder of the clan, Ya'qub Cattaoui, was the first Egyptian Jew to be granted the title of 'bey', and in the early 1880s he was also made a baron of the Habsburg Empire. After this, mindful of their standing as Austrian aristocrats, the family often styled itself 'von Cattaoui'. Little did the Barons von Cattaoui realize that they were to be instrumental, one day, in providing Elkan Adler with an opportunity to observe an aboriginal feast.

In his account of his stay in Cairo, Adler mentioned the private synagogue of the Cattaouis and their adjoining residence, a magnificent palace that had once belonged to a Pasha. He also included a small anecdote about the current head of the family, Moses Cattaoui.

About six years before Adler's visit, the British had been confronted by an armed uprising led by Ahmed Arabi Pasha, a popular figure, venerated in Egypt to this day. The Egyptians were defeated in 1882, and in the aftermath of the war the British assumed direct control of the country's administration. Soon afterwards the British ambassador in Constantinople, Lord Dufferin, was sent to Cairo to fashion a plan for the 're-habilitation' of the country. The Cattaouis made their mansion available to him for the length of his stay, and in recognition of this service, Queen Victoria later sent Moses Cattaoui her portrait—a token which he treasured, writes Adler, 'with no little pride'.

Adler was given a glimpse of a remarkable document in the Cattaouis' strong-room: the eight-hundred-year-old decree issued by the Caliph, giving possession of the Synagogue of Ben Ezra to its congregation. He also paid a visit to Fustat and was horrified to learn that the Synagogue was soon to be torn down and rebuilt. But otherwise the visit made no great impression on him: his inquiries about the Geniza elicited nothing of significance, and he came to the conclusion that 'nowadays no Hebrew MSS of any importance are to be bought in Cairo.' When he wrote his account of his journey, the Geniza did not so much as earn a mention.

Within a couple of years, just as Adler had been told, the old structure of the Synagogue of Ben Ezra was indeed torn down and the building that stands on the site today was put up in its place. The Geniza must have been disturbed in the process of demolition, for the rapid dispersal of its contents appears to have begun at about that time. The officials of the synagogue and the notoriously canny antiquities dealers of Cairo were clearly well aware that those documents could command good prices on the international market, and through their efforts a large number of documents made their way at this time to libraries in Paris, Frankfurt, London, Vienna and Budapest. The Bodleian Library at Oxford also managed to acquire a large collection of Geniza manuscripts in these years, through the efforts of two members of its staff who were quick to recognize their value.

At Cambridge, on the other hand, the manuscripts went virtually unnoticed. The expert in Hebrew documents in Cambridge then was Dr Solomon Schechter, a scholar of great distinction and a forceful, charismatic man, who also happened to be blessed with a natural warmth of spirit and a great deal of charm. He was sent several documents from the Geniza by a learned Rabbi, the scholarly Solomon Wertheimer of Jerusalem. In a few years Schechter's name was to become more closely linked with the Geniza than any other, but until well into the 1890s he was of the opinion (like many other scholars) that these 'Egyptian fragments' were of little real importance. Rabbi Solomon Wertheimer wrote him several letters begging him to forward the documents to Oxford if he saw no value in them, but his pleas went unheeded: Doctor Schechter had not yet found the time to unpack them from their boxes.

At about this time Elkan Adler must have realized that he had been wrong in his initial assessment, for he returned to Cairo in what was to prove the decisive year in the life of the Geniza, 1896. He took with him letters from his brother, Herman Adler (who was later to become the Chief Rabbi of the British Empire), and was received with great cordiality by the Chief Rabbi of Cairo, Rafaïl ben Shimon ha Cohen, and by his warders, who were none other than the senior members of the Cattaoui family. Between them, they granted Adler permission to enter the Geniza and to carry away a certain quantity of documents of his choice. He was personally conducted to Fustat by the Rabbi Rafaïl and, after spending three or four hours immersed in the chamber, he took away a sackful of documents. The material he gathered that day is now spread over several libraries, and a part of it forms the nucleus of the important collection of the Jewish Theological Seminary of New York.

That very same year, 1896, two Presbyterian women, Agnes S. Lewis and Margaret D. Gibson, returned to England after a visit to Egypt, carrying a small collection of Geniza documents. The women were sisters, identical twins with scholarly inclinations, whose large personal fortunes allowed them to travel widely in the Middle East. They had acquired a good deal of experience in manuscripts and antiquities in the course of their wanderings, and on this occasion they were convinced that some of the documents they had brought back with them were of considerable value.

Back in Cambridge, they picked out two fragments that seemed particularly interesting and took them to Solomon Schechter, the Reader in Talmudics. Schechter agreed to look at them, but chiefly out of politeness, for he was still sceptical about the value of the 'Egyptian fragments'. But it so happened that he was taken completely by surprise. One of the documents immediately caught his interest, and next morning, after examining it in his office, he realized that he had stumbled upon a sensational discovery. In great haste, Schechter sent out a note from the University Library:

Dear Mrs Lewis,

I think we have reason to congratulate ourselves. For the fragment I took with me represents a piece of the original Hebrew of Ecclesiasticus. It is the first time that such a thing was discovered. Please do not speak yet about the matter till tomorrow. I will come to you tomorrow about 11 p.m. and talk over the matter with you how to make the matter known.
In haste and great excitement,

Yours sincerely,
S. Schechter.

Schechter's note is dated 13 May 1896. On that very day, Mrs Lewis sent an announcement of the discovery to the prestigious London journal, *The Academy*. The letter was published three days later, under the title, 'Discovery of a Fragment of Ecclesiasticus in the Original Hebrew' and it began: 'All students of the Bible and of the Apocrypha will be interested to learn that, among some fragments of Hebrew MSS which my sister Mrs.

Gibson and I have just acquired in Palestine a leaf of the Book of Ecclesiasticus has been discovered to-day by Mr S. Schechter, lecturer in Talmudic to the University of Cambridge.'

In his own preliminary report published in a learned journal called the *Expositor* later the same year, Schechter announced that he had found a part of the original text of Ecclesiasticus (The Book of Wisdom) by Jesus Ben Siraḥ, which was known to have been written in about 200BC: the original Hebrew had been lost centuries earlier and the book had survived only in Greek translation. 'If it could be proved,' he wrote, 'that Sirach, who flourished in about 200BC composed his work, as some believe, in the Rabbinic idiom...then between Ecclesiasticus and the books of the Old Testament there must lie centuries, nay there must lie, in most cases, the deep waters of the Captivity...'

Neither of the announcements mentioned the Geniza of Fustat as the source of the document: the discovery had so excited Schechter that he had already begun thinking of travelling to Cairo to acquire whatever remained of the documents. Secrecy was essential if the plan was to succeed. He quickly succeeded in enlisting the support of Doctor Charles Taylor, the Master of St John's College, Cambridge. Taylor was a mathematician but he took a keen interest in Rabbinic studies and he persuaded the University to exercise its considerable influence on Schechter's behalf. Schechter left in December 1896, taking with him a letter of recommendation for the Chief Rabbi of Cairo from Herman Adler, then the Chief Rabbi of England, and a 'beautifully ribboned and sealed credential' from the Vice-Chancellor of Cambridge, addressed to the president of the Jewish community of Cairo.

The times could not have been more propitious for Schechter's visit. The British administration in Egypt was then presided over by Sir Evelyn Baring, later Lord Cromer. Known to his subordinates as Over-Baring, he had served in various administrative posts in India and Egypt, and had found little reason to be enthusiastic about the abilites of their modern inhabitants. So little did he think of Egyptians that once, upon hearing a famous Egyptian singer singing a song that went 'My love is lost, O! People find him for me', he is known to have commented that it was typical of Egyptians to expect to have somebody else look for their loves. He expressed his opinions trenchantly in an essay entitled 'The Government of the Subject Races': 'We need not always inquire too closely what these people, who are all, nationally speaking, more or less in statu pupillari, themselves think is best in their own interests…it is essential that each special issue should be decided mainly with reference to what, by the light of Western knowledge and experience…we conscientiously think is best for the subject race.'

Under Lord Cromer's supervision British officials were moved into key positions in every branch of the country's administration. Thus, by the time Schechter arrived in Cairo, a beribboned letter from the Vice-Chancellor of Cambridge University was no mere piece of embossed stationery: it was the backroom equivalent of an imperial edict.

Schechter was fortunate in that Cromer himself took an interest in the success of his mission. The precise details of what transpired between Schechter and British officialdom and the leaders of Cairo's Jewish community are hazy, but soon enough the Chief Rabbi of Cairo and Joseph M. Cattaoui Pasha came to a decision that seems little less than astonishing, in retrospect. They decided to make Solomon Schechter a present of their community's—and their city's—heritage; they granted him permission to remove everything he wanted from the Geniza, every last paper and parchment, without condition or payment.

It has sometimes been suggested that Schechter succeeded so easily in his mission because the custodians of the Synagogue of Ben Ezra had no idea of the real value of the Geniza documents —a species of argument that was widely used in the nineteenth century to justify the acquisition of historical artefacts by colonial powers. In fact, considering that there had been an active and lucrative trade in Geniza documents for several years before Schechter's visit, the beadles and petty officials of the Synagogue could not have been ignorant of their worth. And impoverished as they were, it is hard to believe that they would willingly have parted with a treasure which was, after all, the last remaining asset left to them by their ancestors. In all likelihood the decision was taken for them by the leaders of their community, and they were left with no alternative but acquiescence. As for those leaders, the motives for their extraordinary generosity are not hard to divine: like the élites of so many other groups in the colonized world, they evidently decided to seize the main chance at a time when the balance of power—the ships and the guns— lay overwhelmingly with England.

Schechter, however, took nothing for granted: all the while that he was working in Fustat he took care to cultivate the leaders of the Jewish community in Cairo. He was a man of considerable wit, and he described his relations with the Chief Rabbi and his family with characteristic pithiness in his letters to his wife. Of his manner of dealing with the Rabbi's brother, who had become his advisor, he wrote: 'I flirted with him for hours, and am taking Arabic lessons three times a week. You see how practical your old man is.' He also decided to take the Chief Rabbi to the Pyramids which, remarkably, he had not seen: 'It will cost me about ten shillings, but that is the only way to make yourself popular.' The Rabbi was so charmed that in a later letter Schechter was moved to remark: 'The Rabbi is very kind to me and kisses me on the mouth, which is not very pleasant...'

Other members of the community did not merit quite the same degree of cordiality. Of the custodians of the synagogue, Schechter wrote, in a letter home: 'For weeks and weeks I had to swallow...the annoyance of those scoundrel beadles whom I have to Baksheesh.' Describing his experiences at leisure later, he was to write: 'The whole population within the precincts of the Synagogue were constantly coming forward with claims on my liberality—the men as worthy colleagues employed in the same work [of selection] as myself...the women for greeting me respectfully when I entered the place, or for showing me their deep sympathy in my fits of coughing caused by the dust. If it were a fête day, such as the New Moon or the eve of Sabbath, the amount expected from me for all these kind attentions was much larger, it being only proper that the Western millionaire should contribute from his fortune to the glory of the next meal.'

It must be counted as one of the remarkable features of that age that it could induce Schechter, an otherwise kindly and humane man, himself a member of a family of impoverished Romanian Hasidim, to use a species of language that would have been immediately familiar to any British colonial official. Yet Schechter was writing of his own co-religionists, and moreover of the very group who had sustained the Geniza for almost a thousand years, and whose extraordinary achievement he was then engaged in appropriating. Lord Cromer would probably have expressed himself in more forthright language, but he would have been in complete sympathy with a view of the world in which the interests of the powerful defined necessity, while the demands of the poor appeared as greed.

Schechter had to work for several weeks inside the Geniza chamber, sorting out its contents with the help of the 'scoundrel beadles'. The documents inside were of many different kinds and only a small portion of them had a religious content, properly speaking. But the people who used the Geniza would not have countenanced the modern distinction between the 'secular' and the 'religious': for them there was little that fell outside the scope of God's work, no matter whether it had to do with marriage, prayer or porterage contracts. The Geniza did, in fact, contain innumerable Scriptural and rabbinic documents of great importance, Biblical manuscripts in particular. But it was neither a religious library nor an archive: it was a place where the members of the congregation would throw all the papers in their possession, including letters, bills, contracts, poems, marriage deeds and so on. Often the same piece of paper would contain several different writings, for paper was expensive in the Middle Ages, and people were thrifty in its use. These bits and pieces were thrown haphazardly into the Geniza, and over the centuries the people who occasionally cast their hands into the chamber disarranged them even more. To complicate matters further, large quantities of printed matter and books were also deposited in the Geniza from the sixteenth century onwards.

Schechter eventually decided to leave behind the printed fragments and take only the written ones. He filled about thirty sacks and boxes with the materials and with the help of the British Embassy in Cairo he shipped them off to Cambridge. A few months later he returned himself—laden, as Elkan Adler was to put it, 'with the spoils of the Egyptians'.

In 1898 the manuscripts that Schechter had brought back

from Cairo were formally handed over to the University Library, where they have remained ever since, well-tended and cared for, grouped together as the Taylor-Schechter Collection. The collection contains about a hundred and forty thousand fragments and is the largest single store of Geniza material in the world. It is in this collection, spread over a few dozen documents, that the stories of Abraham Ben Yiju and his slave are preserved —tiny threads, woven into the borders of a gigantic tapestry.

Other hoards of documents, very similar to the Geniza material, were discovered in the Jewish cemetery in Fustat at the turn of the century and then again a decade or so later. Within a few years they too had reached Europe and America, a large part of them going into private collections.

By the First World War, the Geniza had finally been emptied of all its documents. In its home country however, nobody took the slightest notice of its dispersal. In some profound sense, the Islamic high culture of Masr had never really noticed, never found a place for the parallel history the Geniza represented, and its removal only confirmed a particular vision of the past.

Thus, having come to Fustat from the far corners of the known world, a second history of travel carried the documents even further. The irony is that for the most part they went to countries which would have long since destroyed the Geniza had it been a part of their own history. Now it was Masr, which had sustained the Geniza for almost a millennium, that was left with no trace of its riches: not a single scrap or shred of paper to remind her of that aspect of her past.

It was as though the borders that were to divide Palestine several decades later had already been drawn, through time rather than territory, to allocate a choice of Histories.

11

I CAME BACK to Lataifa a week before the end of Ramadan. In my bag I had a few gifts—an illuminated copy of the Qur'an for Shaikh Musa, a leather wallet for Jabir, a ball for the boys' soccer team, and so on. I arrived standing in the back of a pick-up truck, at a time of evening when the boys and young men of the hamlet were always to be found sitting beside the main road, talking with their friends. Some of them ran towards me as soon as I climbed out of the truck. I waved, but to my surprise they neither smiled nor waved back. I noticed that their faces were unusually solemn, and suddenly I was stricken with apprehension.

'Something terrible has happened while you were away, ya mister,' said the first boy to reach me.

'What?'

'You remember Shaikh Musa's son, Hasan?' he said.

'Yes.'

'He's dead; he died a few days ago.'

'He was buried just the other day,' one of the other boys said. 'There was a big ceremony and everything. You missed it.'

Later that evening I went to see Shaikh Musa, carrying the present I had bought for him in Cairo. I wasn't sure whether this would be the right moment to give it to him, but I took it along anyway, because I didn't want to turn up empty-handed at his house.

I was met at the door by his son Ahmed. He was wearing a crumpled jallabeyya and he looked exhausted, with dark circles under his eyes. I shook his hand and uttered the customary phrases of mourning. Whispering the responses, he led me into the guest-room.

Shaikh Musa was sitting in a corner. The room was dark; all

the windows were shut and the lamp had not been lit. He rose to his feet with some difficulty and mumbled the usual words of greeting: 'Welcome, how are you,' and so on, just as he would have if I had dropped in for a casual chat about cotton farming. I said the conventional words of consolation and then tried to add something of my own. 'It's terrible news,' I said. 'I was very shocked...'

He acknowledged this only with a gesture and for a while the three of us sat in silence. As my eyes grew accustomed to the dark I saw that he was unshaven, with several days stubble showing white against his dark skin. He seemed to have aged terribly since I had last seen him: he looked as though he'd shrivelled and withered; his jallabeyya had suddenly outgrown him.

When I handed him the package I had brought with me he acknowledged it only with a slight inclination of his head. Ahmed took it from him, mumbling a word of thanks, and a moment later he left the room.

After we had been alone for a while, Shaikh Musa said softly: 'He was ill when you saw him; you saw how he had that pain in his head that night. It got a little better so he went back to his camp. But then it took a turn for the worse and he had to go into the military hospital. Ahmed visited him there, and I would have gone as well, but Ahmed came back and said that it was all right, he would be well soon, the doctors had said not to worry. And then one night, we had news that he had died. It was very late, the time of the suhur, but we hired a truck from the next village and I and one of my brothers set off at once for Mansourah. When we got there we found that his officers and fellow soldiers were sitting up, keeping vigil beside his body. The army even gave us a car to bring the body back, and the officers and soldiers came too, so that they could attend his funeral.'

'What happened to him?' I asked. 'What sort of illness was it?'

A look of puzzlement came into his eyes as he turned to look at me. 'He was ill,' he said. 'He had a pain in his head; you saw how his head was bandaged.'

My question seemed cruel and I did not persist with it. We sat in silence for a while, and then his two young grandchildren came into the room with their schoolbooks and an oil lamp. They opened their books to study, but in a few minutes something distracted them and they began to play instead. To my relief I saw a slight smile appear on Shaikh Musa's face.

'If you had been here at the time,' he said, 'you would have seen his funeral and the mourning-reception afterwards. So many people came to mourn with us...'

'If only I'd known,' I said. 'I'd have come back at once.'

He looked down at his feet and fell silent. I wanted to tell him my big news, that Dr Issa had arranged for me to leave Abu-'Ali's house, to move out of Lataifa, to Nashawy. But the moment did not seem appropriate, and in a while I got up to leave.

'He was so young,' Shaikh Musa said. 'And his health was always so good.'

He rose to his feet, and when his face was level with mine I saw that he was weeping. 'Al-duniya zayy kida,' he said helplessly. 'The world is like that...' He went quickly back inside after seeing me out, and I turned and walked away.

So it happened that I never kept the promise I had made to tell him about Masr.

12

I LEFT EGYPT in 1981, and it was not until seven years later that circumstances permitted me to begin a serious inquiry into the story of the Slave of MS H.6: in the ten years that had passed since I first came across Goitein's brief reference to Abraham Ben Yiju and his Slave, my path had crossed theirs again and again, sometimes by design and sometimes inadvertently, in North Africa, Egypt and the Malabar, until it became clear that I could no longer resist the logic of those coincidences.

I started upon the Slave's trail hoping that I would be able to ask for guidance from Goitein himself: I took encouragement from an article published in India, in 1963, in which he had tried to interest Indians in the Geniza. But I soon discovered, to my great disappointment, that he had died in 1985, at the age of eighty-five. The only alternative left was to start by going through Goitein's work and tracking the Slave through references to Abraham Ben Yiju.

The blitheness of that beginning did not long survive the discovery of the enormity of that task. The complete bibliography of Goitein's writings runs into a seventy-page book, with a twenty-two page supplement. It contains a total of 666 entries in Hebrew, German, English and French. His writings were published in Europe, America, Israel, Tunisia, India and Pakistan, and they included pieces in popular magazines, a Hebrew play and, of course, innumerable books and articles. At the age of thirty Goitein had started single-handed upon the kind of project for which university departments usually appoint committees: an edition of the *Ansâb al-Ashrâf,* (The Noble Lineages), a 2,500 page work by the ninth-century Arab historian, al-Balâdhuri. His interest in the Geniza had begun with a visit to Budapest in 1948 and had continued through the rest of his life. His monumental study, based on his Geniza research, *A Mediterranean Society*, was acclaimed as a landmark in medieval scholarship as soon as the first of its five volumes appeared in 1967. It was to establish him as possibly the greatest of the Geniza scholars, the pioneering researcher without whose labours an inquiry into the lives of Ben Yiju and the Slave of MS H.6 would not be possible today.

Scanning through the relevant parts of Goitein's oeuvre, I discovered that his interest lay, on the whole, in the broad sweep of history, so that the references to individuals, such as Ben Yiju, were scattered randomly through his writings like the windblown trail of a paperchase. Some of those references led to the work of other scholars, such as E. Strauss, who had first edited the letter of MS H.6. Others pencilled in the outlines of Ben Yiju's career, in passing, while pointing in two further directions: on the one hand to certain specific Geniza documents, and on the other to one of Goitein's own unfinished works, a project which he had named 'the India Book'.

The references to this work began in the 1950s not long after Goitein first started working with the Geniza documents. His researches had led him to a large number of letters and other manuscripts referring to the trade between the Indian Ocean and the Mediterranean. He soon conceived of a plan to publish them as a collection, under the title of *The India Book*, but as his work proceeded he found ever-increasing quantities of material, and the project was continually deferred, while other aspects of his research took precedence. *The India Book* was never abandoned however: he announced that the book would contain about three hundred documents, and in 1964 he even published the catalogue numbers of those documents, including those that referred to Ben Yiju, as a guide to other researchers. But despite his announced intentions, the book was still unfinished when he died in 1985, in Princeton.

The road now led directly to Princeton University, where Goitein had taught for many years: I was told that his colleagues and students in the Department of Near Eastern Studies had compiled an archive of his papers there. Eventually I went to visit the archive myself but a disappointment awaited me there: I found that access to most of his papers on the India trade was restricted because an edition of his notes for the projected *India Book* was in preparation, although it was unlikely to be published within the next several years. From the papers that I was allowed to see, I had the impression that Goitein had in fact already published most of his information regarding Ben Yiju's life in scattered bits and pieces, for much of the material was already familiar from my earlier reading.

At the end of the visit it was clear to me that there was only one way forward now, and that was to go to the Geniza documents themselves, directly to Ben Yiju's own papers. But across that road lay a seemingly impassable barrier: the obstacle of language.

Ben Yiju's documents were mostly written in an unusual, hybrid language: one that has such an arcane sound to it that it might well be an entry in a book of Amazing Facts. It is known today as Judæo-Arabic; it was a colloquial dialect of medieval Arabic, written in the Hebrew script.

Judæo-Arabic evolved after Muslim armies, recruited mainly from the Arabian peninsula, conquered most of the Middle East and North Africa in the seventh century. The language of the conquerors soon came to supplant the other languages of the empire, including Aramaic, the language then generally in use among the Jews of those regions. But of course, Jews continued to use Hebrew for religious purposes and, in time, when they started writing in their newly adopted tongue, it was in the sanctified alphabet of their Scriptures.

From this odd smelting came an alloy that had its own distinct sheen and texture, with little resemblance to the language written by Muslim Arabs. Written Arabic, in its usual form, is the literary variety of the language and is more or less standard throughout the Arab world, from Morocco to Iraq. Spoken Arabic, on the other hand, varies so much from region to region that the speech of an Iraqi is almost incomprehensible to a Moroccan. A great gulf separates the two registers of Arabic, the formal, literary language, and the slangy, regional dialects: for all practical purposes they are separate languages, with their own distinct vocabularies and grammars.

Judæo-Arabic, determinedly contrary, was not like either form of Arabic: unlike the dialects, it was a written language, and unlike written Arabic, it had the vocabulary and grammar of the spoken language. It was in a way something much simpler than either form of Arabic: a representation of colloquial speech in writing. But since colloquial Arabic has always varied between regions, Judæo-Arabic too tended to take on somewhat different colours in different parts of the Arab world. The language of the Geniza documents, for example, has a strong flavour of North African Arabic, since so many members of the community were from that region.

But although Judæo-Arabic was much closer to the spoken language than literary Arabic, it was not uniformly colloquial. The people who used it would often try to introduce Arabic classicisms into their written language, with varying degrees of success. Often they would use words and spellings which would have startled well-educated Muslim Arabs, but which they took to be elegant usage. Eight centuries later, those odd solecisms often have an awkward, endearingly human grace, where the correct form would seem merely formal or stilted.

At the same time, everyone who wrote Judæo-Arabic had a thorough knowledge of the Hebrew Scriptures, and though they were not usually able to use Hebrew as a language of expression, they were well able to quote in it. Thus their prose is studded with Hebrew proverbs and long passages from the bible, as well as legal and religious terms from the archaic language Aramaic.

When I first read about it, Judæo-Arabic sounded bafflingly esoteric: it is not easy, after all, to see oneself sitting down to leaf through a collection of eight-hundred-year-old documents, written in a colloquial dialect of medieval Arabic, transcribed in the Hebrew script, and liberally strewn with Hebrew and Aramaic. At its easiest, Arabic is very difficult for a foreigner, and such knowledge as I had of it was mainly of the dialect spoken around Lataifa: a broad, peasant tongue, so earthy that my accent would often earn sniffs from waiters in Cairo restaurants and provoke shopkeepers to ask to see my money before they reached for their shelves. Those experiences had given me something of the fellah's diffidence about his language: it would never have occurred to me that this simple, rustic dialect could be of any use in so rarified a domain of erudition as the reading of twelfth-century Judæo-Arabic manuscripts.

Worse was still to come, for I soon discovered that there was no accepted method of learning to read the manuscripts except through a long apprenticeship with one of the handful of scholars who had made a lifetime's speciality of the subject. The only other means was to take copies of those documents that had been published, and to compare them with the actual folio pages—

103

smudged, worn eight-hundred-year-old bits of paper—until such time as one's eyes grew expert in deciphering the script.

At that point I almost gave up, but just then, when all the tunnels on the road seemed finally to have closed, a short conversation with one of the foremost experts in the field, Mark Cohen, a one-time student of Goitein's, and custodian of his archive at Princeton, gave me pause. The language was not as difficult as it seemed, Mark Cohen told me; Hebrew characters were easy to learn, and once the writing had been deciphered, the Arabic itself was fairly simple. It was the deciphering of the documents, rather than the language itself, that was the hard part: the language would not present a particular problem to someone who knew colloquial Arabic. The palæography, on the other hand, the deciphering of the texts, was often extremely difficult, yet many students had been known to grow quickly adept at it. Of course, I would never be equipped to produce authoritative editions of Geniza texts, but it was perfectly possible, if I worked hard at the palæography and learnt to decipher and transcribe the documents, that I would be able to deal with them well enough to follow the stories of the Slave of MS H.6 and Abraham Ben Yiju.

Mark Cohen's encouragement made up my mind: I decided I couldn't give up without trying.

To my surprise I found that he was right, that the Hebrew script was indeed much easier to decipher than cursive Arabic since the letters stood apart, each by itself. Soon enough, I made other surprising discoveries. I found that some of the usages of the dialect of Lataifa were startlingly close to those of the North African Arabic spoken by Ben Yiju; that far from being useless the dialect of Lataifa and Nashawy had given me an invaluable skill.

Over the next couple of years, as I followed the Slave's trail from library to library, there were times when the magnifying glass would drop out of my hand when I came upon certain words and turns of phrase for I would suddenly hear the voice of Shaikh Musa speaking in the documents in front of me as clearly as though I had been walking past the canal, on my way between Lataifa and Nashawy.

NASHÂWY

1

IN DECEMBER 1988, when I was at last hot upon the Slave's trail, I went back to visit Lataifa. It was almost eight years since I had left Egypt.

It was cold and wintry the day I left Cairo, with rain hanging down in thin sheets from a cloud-corded sky. By the time I reached Damanhour night had fallen and the streets were clogged with shoals of churned mud. I had wanted to get there in the afternoon, on one of the old Hungarian trains, where the seats had cushioned foot-rests and the attendants served elaborate meals on trays. I had imagined myself watching the familiar sights roll past my window while I ate my lunch, just as I used to all those years ago, when the railway's fried chicken had tasted richly of metropolitan excitement after weeks of village fare.

But by the time I reached Ramses Station it was too late in the morning: all the tickets were sold for the day.

I'd wanted to be there early, but I had spent the first part of the morning running feverishly between shops, wondering whether I had enough presents in my bag, stopping to buy a pen there and a wallet here and adding to my store of scarves, lighters and watches. That had been pretty much the pattern of my days ever since I arrived in Cairo. Every day, upon waking, I'd told myself that I would go to Lataifa that very morning, and every time I had found some excuse to put it off. No one was waiting for me, after all: I had not written ahead to tell anyone of my visit. My correspondence with Lataifa and Nashawy, once frequent, had become increasingly irregular and then ceased altogether. It was now almost three years since I had last received a letter from Egypt. I had no idea of what to expect, who was doing what, who was alive and who dead: the years in between were a chasm of darkness between me and a brilliantly floodlit corner of my memory.

Since all the trains were full, I had no option but to go over to the other side of Ramses Station and take a share-taxi with eight other people. 'The world's awash with rain,' said the man sitting next to me, as we set off: it was a bad day to go into the countryside; there'd been rain all through the week and the village roads had probably turned into swamps. The Datsun trucks probably wouldn't be able to get through; nobody could get through that kind of mud, nobody except the fellaheen, sitting on their donkeys. I had better be prepared to spend the night in Damanhour; it wasn't likely that I would be able to go any further.

But when we reached Damanhour he walked with me to the truck-stop and helped me get a place on the last truck heading in the direction of Nashawy. The driver made room for me in his cabin, but he wasn't eager to venture far into the countryside in such weather. As soon as we had set off, he said: 'I can't go as far as Nashawy. The road's a river of mud out there.'

'What about Lataifa?' I asked. 'Can you get as far as that?'

'Let's see,' he said, grudgingly. 'I don't know.'

Within a few minutes we had left the town behind and were

speeding down a narrow, deserted road. I had tried to imagine this moment for years: the drive from Damanhour to Lataifa and Nashawy. In my mind I had always seen a bright, sunlit day, the canal beside the road glittering under a blue sky while children played naked in the water and women walked towards the town balancing baskets of vegetables on their heads. The scene was so vivid in my mind that even in the imagining my stomach had often knotted in excitement. But now, travelling down that road after so many years I felt no excitement at all, only an old, familiar sensation, one that had always accompanied me on my way back from Damanhour, no matter whether I'd been away an hour or a week: the lassitude of homecoming mixed with a quiet sense of dread.

Most of the truck's passengers got down at the first stop, a small market town, a good distance from Lataifa. It was late now, well after the evening prayers, and the main street was deserted. All the shops were shut and there were no lights anywhere except for a few flickering lamps. Once we were past the town, the truck began to yaw and skid on the ridges of mud the rain had carved into the road. The villages around us were eerily dark, and as we crawled past them, packs of dogs came racing after the truck, snapping savagely at the tyres. The other passengers got off in ones and twos along the way, and soon I was alone in the cabin with the driver.

The driver was nervous now, unsettled by the darkness and the howling dogs. He lit a cigarette, holding the wheel steady with his elbow, and cast me a sidelong glance. 'Whose house are you going to in Lataifa?' he asked.

'Shaikh Musa's,' I said. 'Do you know him?'

'No,' he shook his head. 'La.' In front of us, half the road seemed to have dissolved into the canal which ran beside it.

'I don't know if we can go on for long,' said the driver. All that was visible ahead through the shimmering rain-drenched windscreen was a small patch of road lit by the headlights.

'How will you find the house in this darkness?' the driver asked. 'Everyone's asleep—no one can show you the way.'

'I know the house,' I said. 'If you stop where I tell you, I'll be able to find it.'

'How do you know the house?' He was suddenly curious. 'Aren't you a foreigner? Why are you going there all alone so late at night?'

I explained how I'd been brought to Lataifa by my Professor at the University of Alexandria, but his nerves were on edge and the story only served to arouse his suspicion.

'Why did they bring you here?' he said sharply. 'Why here, and what was it that you were doing exactly?'

I tried to reassure him as best I could, but my Arabic had become rusty in the years that I had been away, and my halting explanations only served to deepen his suspicions further.

'I'll come with you to the house you're going to,' he said, glaring into the windscreen. 'Just to make sure you find it.'

'And you will be welcome,' I said, hoping that he was not one of those people who were disposed to carry tales to the police. 'You will bring blessings with you. It's not much further now.'

Suddenly I saw Lataifa's little mosque on the left, through the driver's window. 'There,' I said, pointing ahead. 'Stop—I'll get off there.'

He stamped too hard on the brakes, inadvertently, and the truck skidded across the wet mud and came to a halt with its nose poised over the edge of the canal. Climbing out gingerly, I stepped back from the edge, squelching heavily through the mud. When next I looked up I saw a slight, ghostly figure in the distance: a boy in a jallabeyya, leaning against a wall, under an overhang, watching me. For a moment I was certain it was Jabir and I almost shouted out aloud: in the reflected glow of the headlights he seemed to have the same blunt, rounded features, as well as the ruddy complexion of all the Latifs. But it took only that moment to remind me that I was thinking of a Jabir I had known eight years ago, when the figure in the shadows would have been a seven- or eight-year-old boy.

I shifted my feet awkwardly in the mud, and then, raising my hand, I said: 'Al-salâm 'aleikum.' My tongue was suddenly heavy, weighted with an unexpected shyness.

"Aleikum al-salam,' he said, responding in full. 'Wa raḥmatullâhî wa barâkâtu.'

The truck suddenly started up again and came to a halt between us, engine roaring.

'Hey, boy,' the driver shouted. 'Who's Shaikh Musa? Do you know him?'

The boy stepped forward and looked into the driver's window. 'Yes,' he said, in the gruff, surly voice which the boys of the village kept for townspeople.

'Where's his house?'

'There.' The boy pointed down the lane.

'Good, let's go,' said the driver. He stepped out of the truck and kicked his feet, to dislodge the long tentacles of mud that had attached themselves to his shoes.

'Come on, yalla,' he said, in irritation. 'I want to talk to this man, this Shaikh Musa.'

Halfway down the lane the boy fell in beside me. 'I know you,' he said, smiling in surprise. 'You used to come to our house when I was little and you used to walk in the fields when we were out picking cotton.'

I looked at him carefully, trying to remember his name, but of course, he'd been a child when I had last seen him, and at that time I was myself of an age when I had hardly noticed children. Before I could ask him his father's name he came to a stop and gestured at Shaikh Musa's door. The house was in complete darkness. I could not see so much as a chink of light behind the door or between the shutters of the windows. The boy saw me hesitating and gave me a nudge, pointing at the door.

Scraping the mud carefully off my shoes, I went up to the door and knocked. A long time seemed to pass before a voice answered, asking: 'Who's there?' It was a woman's voice and it seemed to echo all the way down the lane.

'Ana,' I said stupidly, my legs oddly unsteady, and that very instant Shaikh Musa's voice began to roar—'Amitab, ya Amitab, ya doktór, where have you been?'—and for all the time it took his wife to undo the latch he kept repeating: 'Amitab, ya Amitab, where have you been?' When the door was open at last we brought our hands together with a great resounding slap and shook them hard, first one, and then both together, and all the while he kept saying—'where have you been all this time? where were you?'—but there were tears in his eyes now, as there were in mine, and so it was not until months afterwards that it occurred to me to wonder how he had recognized my voice when all I had said in answer to his wife's question was 'It's me'.

The driver stepped up to Shaikh Musa and shook his hand. 'So you know him?' he asked with a nod in my direction, smiling a little sheepishly.

'Yes,' Shaikh Musa laughed. 'Yes, we all know him here.'

'That's all right then,' the driver said, turning to leave. 'I just wanted to make sure that he reached you safely.'

'Come in and have some tea with us,' Shaikh Musa shouted

after him, but he was already gone, stamping noisily down the lane.

Shaikh Musa's wife ushered us into the guest-room, out of the rain, showing us the way with a kerosene lamp. 'You sit here and talk,' she said. 'I'll bring you some tea and food in a couple of minutes.'

Placing the lamp on a window-sill, she gave its sooty glass chimney a rub with her sleeve. 'We hardly bother to clean our lamps any more,' she said, 'we have electricity now. It's just fate that you should arrive in the middle of a power cut.'

'Everything's changed in all these years that you've been away,' said Shaikh Musa. 'All this time I used to say to myself, the doktór will come back one day, he will come back soon, everyone comes back to Masr; they have to, because Masr is the Mother of the World.'

His wife gave the lamp a final scrub and opened the door. 'Do you know?' she said, as the cold wind whistled in, shaking the flame. 'He used to ask about you every day. "Where's the doktór al-Hindi? Where is he? What is he doing?" Every day he used to ask.'

There was a long moment of silence when she left the room. Shaikh Musa sat on the divan with a leg crossed under him, watching the flame with a gently quizzical smile: except for a few wrinkles at the corner of his mouth, he was completely unchanged.

Then, raising his eyes, he pointed to a framed photograph hanging on the wall, an enlargement of the picture of his son Hasan that he had always carried in his wallet. 'I had this big one made in Damanhour,' he said. 'In a studio near the railway station.'

He had hung it beside his own picture, taken when he was a

young man serving his draft in the army. They were very alike, father and son, both in uniform, Shaikh Musa in a peaked cap and Hasan in combat fatigues.

'You were away in Masr when he died,' he said. 'When you came back the mourning ceremony was already over.'

He looked down at the floor, fingering his worry-beads with the slow, deliberate gesture that had become inseparably linked with him in my memory.

'All the officers came,' he said. 'The officers and all the soldiers in his unit. They all came and we had a Quran-reader from Damanhour. But by the time you came back it was all over.'

Then, unaccountably, his eyes lit up and he jumped to his feet and opened the door. 'Wait a moment,' he said, and hurried out of the room. He was back in a few minutes, carrying an ornamented box in his hands. Setting it reverently upon the divan he turned to me: 'Do you know what this is?'

I was unsure for a moment, but then suddenly I remembered.

'It's the Quran al-Sharif you brought for me from Masr,' he said. He opened the lid and took a long look at the cover.

'It was after Hasan's death,' he said. 'You came back from Masr, and afterwards you said you were leaving Lataifa and going away to Nashawy.'

2

EVEN AFTER I had gone to live in Nashawy, eight years before, it was always Shaikh Musa I came to visit when I had questions to ask. Shaikh Musa had known Nashawy well once, when he was younger, and his memory was still crammed with stories about its inhabitants: when we talked he would sometimes surprise himself by recalling an incident or a detail from fifteen or twenty years ago. Thinking back later, it often seemed to me that we had created a village of our own during those conversations, between the two of us.

Most of his memories dated back at least a decade, for with his advancing years, the one and a half miles to Nashawy had come to seem like an increasingly formidable distance and he rarely went there except to attend an old friend's funeral or a relative's wedding. The only reason why he was still able to keep up with Nashawy at all was because so many people came to visit him in his own house. That was why he enjoyed our conversations as much as I did: he liked to hear the news and keep in touch.

It was in the early days, when I first moved to Nashawy, that I was most regular in my visits to Shaikh Musa in Lataifa. He would ask me questions about who I'd met and what I'd been doing, and then he would give me advice about the people I would do best to avoid and who I ought to seek out. It was he, for instance, who first told me about Imam Ibrahim.

They were both of the same age, he told me, but you wouldn't believe it now if you saw them together, Imam Ibrahim looked so much older. Not many people knew of him now, because he lived in seclusion and didn't go out very much, but as a young man, his name had been well-known throughout the area: people had said of him that he had the gift of baraka.

It so happened that Imam Ibrahim belonged to one of the two founding families of Nashawy, a lineage called Abu-Kanaka. The other was the Badawy: they were the first two families to come and settle in the area. They had not been there very long,

117

for Nashawy was not an old village by Egyptian standards: in fact, only a few generations ago the land around it had been a part of the great desert to the west. It was only after the Mahmudiya Canal was completed in 1820, linking Cairo and Alexandria, that the area was brought under the plough. But even then it was a wilderness for a long time, without people or settlements.

Then one day, two young men had set off westwards from a village in the interior, looking for land and a good new place to settle. One of those men was of Bedouin origin: his ancestors had once wandered as far afield as Libya and Tunisia, but in time, tiring of the nomadic life, they had abandoned the desert for the sown. They had settled in the Delta, where for many generations their descendants worked on the land as fellaheen, until all that remained to remind them of their Bedouin past was the name of their lineage—al-Badawy.

The other young settler was from a lineage of barbers and healers, a family called Abu-Kanaka whose members were well known throughout the region for their zeal in religious matters and for their skill in the arts of healing. The Abu-Kanaka youth who set out on that westward journey had a fine reputation, despite his tender years: all the world knew him to be a model of goodness and piety, as well as a skilled and knowledgeable healer.

So the two young men had set out from their native village, and after a long and difficult journey they reached the area around Nashawy. There was nothing there then, no houses or canals or fields, but the Abu-Kanaka youth had declared that he could feel in his heart that the land had baraka and they had decided to settle there. Soon the young Badawy man acquired some land and began to raise crops. As the years passed more and more of his kinsmen came out from their native village and they too bought land and built houses in Nashawy. Before long the village was so full of Badawy families that they came to be known as the pre-eminent lineage of the village, the 'aṣl al-balad'. Later people of many other lineages settled in Nashawy, but right until the Revolution of 1952 it was the Badawy who owned most of the land and it was always a Badawy who was the chief official, the 'omda of the village.

The young Abu-Kanaka man, on the other hand, bought no land at all: he earned his living by healing and cutting people's hair, as his family had always done—a humble man, with a modest house and a small family. But at the same time, his renown as a good person and a man of religion continued to grow, and when at last a mosque was built in Nashawy, he was made the Imam, the caretaker and the leader of the prayers. Such was the respect in which he was held that his son inherited the position after him and his lineage held it ever afterwards. When he died he was universally mourned and the people of the village built him a special grave, right next to the canal. Later, he even came to be acknowledged as the guardian saint of the village.

When he was a young man, Shaikh Musa said, there were many who thought that Imam Ibrahim Abu-Kanaka had taken after his famous ancestor. He had shown remarkable skill in curing the sick, for example; there was a shelf in his house that was lined with texts on medicine, and everyone knew that he was very learned in the classical arts of healing. He had soon acquired a reputation as a healer who could do miracles with his herbs and roots, and he had had patients from all the surrounding villages. He had also become known for his learning in the scriptures, and at one time he had been much sought after for his opinions on points of theology and matters of religious law and jurisprudence.

'You must make sure to meet him,' said Shaikh Musa. 'He's well read in history and religion and many other things and there's a lot you could learn from him.'

But when I asked how I might meet Imam Ibrahim, Shaikh Musa's answer was a sigh and a doubtful shake of his head. He hadn't seen the Imam around for the last so many years, he said, and he heard reports that he kept very much to himself nowadays and rarely went anywhere or met anyone. He had a great many troubles on his head, people said, because he had made an unfortunate second marriage in middle age, and had been tormented by domestic difficulties ever since. His son had now taken over many of his duties, and for the most part he kept to himself, living more or less in seclusion.

'But you must try to meet him,' said Shaikh Musa. 'Ask the other people you meet in Nashawy: they'll be able to tell you about him...'

3

LATER, ON SEVERAL occasions, Shaikh Musa made a point of asking me whether I had talked to anyone about Imam Ibrahim. But as it turned out, when I did eventually have something to tell him, he was taken by surprise: he was not quite prepared for how differently people of a younger generation looked upon the world, even in a place so close to home as Nashawy.

One of the people I had talked to recently was a young

teacher called Ustaz Sabry. Shaikh Musa had never met him himself, but like everyone else in the area he had heard of him, for Ustaz Sabry was rapidly becoming quite a well-known figure in the surrounding villages.

'People say he's an impressive talker,' said Shaikh Musa, pursing his lips. 'But I've also heard it said that he's one of those men whom we call Too-Much-Talk in these parts—has something to say about everything.'

'I can tell you this,' I said, 'he knows a lot. He's read a great deal, and he's one of the best-informed people I've ever met.'

'You must be right,' said Shaikh Musa. But a look of doubt descended on his face as he puffed at his shusha.

Ustaz Sabry had taken me by surprise the very first time I met him.

I had been introduced to him by the headmaster of the school he taught in, the primary school in Nashawy. The headmaster was a friendly, pleasant man in his early forties who had been elevated to his post largely because his father had been headmaster before him. He played the part he had inherited with conscientious diligence but he was at heart too gentle a man to enjoy the authority that came with it. I once watched him caning a boy with a ruler: he had applied himself to the task with such an evident lack of relish that the boy had never once lost his smirk.

In me I think the headmaster hoped to find a source of sympathy for his daily vexations, a connection with the student-world in Alexandria that he had once inhabited himself. In any event, he always went out of his way to be kind to me, inviting me frequently to his house and always sending word the moment a letter addressed to me went astray and ended up on his desk.

It was on one such occasion, when I'd been asked to go to his office to collect a letter, that I first met Ustaz Sabry.

The mid-morning break was in progress when I arrived at the school, and a number of teachers had drifted into the head-master's office to take refuge from the hurricane of screaming children that was whirling through the corridors. I knew several of the teachers already, and the headmaster introduced me to the rest, one by one. Most of them were from Damanhour and other nearby towns, and they were all smartly dressed, the men in jackets and ties and the women in skirts and white nylon scarves. I had been surprised at first, to see how they always arrived in Nashawy looking perfectly turned out, proper effendis, with every hair in place despite the dusty ride from Damanhour; I discovered later that it was their privilege to travel in the drivers' cabins of the trucks that ran through the area—the villagers had given them the right of sanctuary from their lowly dust.

Going around the room, shaking hands, we came to a man who did not seem to belong with the others. He was dressed in a grimy, ink-stained jallabeyya, a barrel-bodied man in his mid-thirties, with thick, liver-coloured lips, and large, watery eyes.

'This is Ustaz Sabry,' said the headmaster. 'He is from Nashawy; his family live at the far end of the village, across the canal from the government clinic. You will have a lot to discuss with him because he is writing a thesis too.'

He put a hand on Ustaz Sabry's shoulder and asked: 'What is it that you're studying exactly?'

Ustaz Sabry flashed me a smile and said something quickly about medieval Egyptian history. His voice had the precise, resonant pitch of that of a man accustomed to addressing large gatherings and when he turned to me and asked what my subject was, I found to my surprise that he spoke in the simple fellah dialect of Nashawy. All the other teachers had educated city accents.

'Anthropology,' I answered, and he responded immediately with another question: 'Social or physical?'

'Social,' I said, and he nodded, smiling: 'Yes, good; that's a bit like history or philosophy, isn't it? Much better than all those bones and skeletons.'

The headmaster was pleased by this exchange. 'I knew you would have a lot to talk about,' he said. He gave me a slap on the back and said: 'You must go and talk to Ustaz Sabry properly. He's read so much he'll be able to tell you about many things.'

Later, after we had exchanged a few remarks about our respective subjects, Ustaz Sabry invited me to visit him at his home that evening, so we could carry on our conversation.

I set off for his house a little before the sunset prayers, and in my eagerness to get there I forgot to find out exactly where he lived. As a result I was soon lost, for Nashawy was much larger than Lataifa, with its houses squeezed close together around a labyrinth of tunnel-like lanes, some of which came to unexpected dead ends while others circled back upon themselves. At the centre of the village was a large, open square where the mosque and the ceremonial 'guest-house' stood, adjoining each other, a modest pair of buildings, neat, square and whitewashed, with the mosque's single minaret rising high above the tousled hayricks that topped the surrounding houses. After I had passed through the square a second time I swallowed my pride and turning to the long train of children who had attached themselves to me, I asked the tallest among them to lead me to Ustaz Sabry's house.

He ran ahead of me and after a couple of turnings he stopped and pointed at a carved door at the corner of two lanes. A communal water-tap stood directly opposite and the teenage girls who had gathered there looked up from their jerrycans and earthen pots as I came around the corner in a cloud of dust, with my train of children rumbling behind me. They watched as I stood in front of the house, looking undecidedly at the heavy wooden door, and soon they began to giggle and make catcalls.

'Come and talk to us, over here.'

'Why so shy, ya Hindi?'

'Wouldn't you like a drink of water?'

I turned my back upon them while the children squealed with laughter, and holding myself stiff and stony-faced I went up and knocked at the door. 'Who's there?' came the response, in a woman's voice, and from across the road one of the girls shouted: 'It's the Hindi.'

The door opened and a woman dressed in the severe black robes of an elderly widow appeared in front of me. 'Yes?' she said, frowning in puzzlement.

'Let him in,' the girls laughed. 'Or he'll run away.'

The woman's head snapped upright, eyes blazing. 'Shut your mouths, you over there,' she shouted. 'Don't you have any shame?'

The girls muttered rebelliously under their breath—'Listen to her, who does she think she is?'—but to my relief their giggles died away.

'Is Ustaz Sabry here?' I asked.

She was watching me closely now, and suddenly, clapping her hands to her thin, fine-boned cheeks, she cried: 'Why, aren't you the doktór al-Hindi? I saw you at the Thursday market last week: tell me, why did you pay fifteen piastres for that little handful of peas? Everyone was talking about it.'

I cast my mind back, but try as I might, I could not remember how much I had paid for my peas.

'You should let 'Amm Taha go to the market for you,' she said. 'Isn't he helping you in your house? He'll know what to do—he knows all about buying and selling.'

'All right,' I said, 'but I'm here now because Ustaz Sabry told me...'

'Welcome, welcome,' she said. 'Please come in, you're welcome, but Ustaz Sabry isn't in just this minute.'

'He isn't here?' I said. 'But he told me...'

Craning her head around, with a considerable effort, she shouted into the interior of the house: 'Where did Sabry go?'

There was no answer, and she turned around again to face me, so slowly that I could almost hear her joints creak. 'He should be back soon,' she said.

Then, all of a sudden her eyes focused brightly on me, and she stretched out a thin, bony finger and tapped me on the shoulder. 'Tell me,' she said. 'Is it true what they say about you? That in your country people burn their dead?'

'Some people do,' I said. 'It depends.'

'Why do they do it?' she cried. 'Don't they know it's wrong? You can't cheat the Day of Judgement by burning your dead.'

'Please,' I said. 'Do you know when Ustaz Sabry is going to be back?'

'Soon,' she said. 'Soon. But now tell me this: is it true that you worship cows? That's what they were saying at the market. They said that just the other day you fell to your knees in front of a cow, right out in the fields in front of everyone.'

'I tripped,' I said, taking a backwards step. 'I'll come back some other time: tell Ustaz Sabry.'

'You have to put a stop to it,' she called out after me as I hurried away down the lane. 'You should try to civilize your people. You should tell them to stop praying to cows and burning their dead.'

4

THE CARETAKER OF the house I had moved into in Nashawy was called Taha. He was a familiar figure around the village, and was known to everyone as Uncle; I never heard anyone address him without adding an 'Amm to his name. He was in his late fifties or thereabouts, excruciatingly thin, slack-mouthed because his lower jaw was not quite in line with the upper, and with one unmoving eye that looked away from the other at a sharp angle, in a fixed, unblinking glare.

Soon after I moved in, he and I reached an arrangement whereby he fetched me a meal from his house once a day: he did several different odd jobs and this was yet another in a long list. He usually came to my room at about midday with my meal, and one day, not long after I had missed Ustaz Sabry at his house, I told him about my abortive visit.

'Amm Taha was not surprised in the least. 'Of course he wasn't there,' he said. 'Ustaz Sabry is a busy man, and if you want to find him at his house you have to go at the right time. What time was it when you went?'

'A little before the sunset prayers,' I told him.

'That's not the time to go,' he said, with a mournful shake of his head. 'At that time he usually goes to one of his friends' houses to watch TV or else he goes to visit people in the next village.'

Startled as I was by the comprehensiveness of his information, I did not need to ask him how he knew; I had learnt already that very little happened in Nashawy without 'Amm Taha being aware of it. As a rule he collected his information in the evenings, when he went around from house to house to see if anyone had eggs or milk or anything else to sell. One of his many professions was that of vendor, and he regularly bought local products in Nashawy and took them elsewhere to sell. Eggs, milk and cheese were his staples, but he wasn't particular: he would just as willingly take a bunch of carrots, or a cauliflower that had escaped the pot the night before, or even a fattened chicken or a rabbit.

Every other day or so, he would gather his gleanings together, load them on his donkey-cart, and drive down the dirt road to Damanhour or to one of the weekly markets in the nearby villages. The profits were meagre and they depended largely on the quality of his information: on whether or not he knew whose cow was in milk and who needed ready cash for their daughter's wedding and would accept a punitive price for a chicken. In other words 'Amm Taha's takings as a vendor hung upon his success in ferreting out some of the most jealously guarded of household secrets: in discovering exactly how matters stood behind the walls and talismans that guarded every house from the envy of neighbours and the Evil Eye. As it happened, 'Amm Taha was unusually successful in his profession because it was mostly women who were the guardians of those secrets, and many amongst them talked to him as they would not have to any other man—in large part, I think, because he did everything he could to let it be known that he was a poor, harmless old man, still childless despite many years of marriage, and too infirm to undertake the sort of exertion that results in procreation.

''Amm Taha keeps an eye on everything,' people would say, 'because one of his eyes looks to the left, while the other watches the right.' 'Amm Taha did nothing to contradict this, nor did he discourage those who claimed to detect an element of the supernatural in his prescience.

Once, 'Amm Taha happened to be in my room when a hoopoe flew in through an open window. The sight of the bird seemed to work an instant transformation in him and he began to race around the room, slamming shut the doors and windows.

'Stop that,' I shouted while the frightened bird flapped its wings against the walls, leaving a trail of droppings on my desk. 'Stop, what are you doing, ya 'Amm Taha?'

'Amm Taha paid no attention; he was half in flight himself, leaping nimbly from the bed to my desk and back, with his hands hooked like talons and the sleeves of his jallabeyya flapping wildly, an albatross swooping on its prey. He knocked the bird to the floor with a wave of his jallabeyya, and after breaking its neck with an expert twist of his hands, he slipped it into his pocket, as matter-of-factly as though it were a ten-piastre note.

I was astonished by this performance for I had often heard people say that hoopoes were 'friends of the fellaheen' and ought not to be harmed because they helped the crops by killing worms. He must have sensed my surprise for he explained hurriedly that it wasn't anything important, it was just that he particularly needed some hoopoe's blood that day.

'Hoopoe's blood?' I said. It was clear that he would rather

have dropped the subject, but I decided to persist. 'What will you do with it?'

'I need it for a spell,' he said brusquely, 'for women who can't bear children.' One of the hoopoe's wings had somehow emerged from his pocket and its tip was hanging out now, like the end of a handkerchief. He tucked it back carefully, and then, after a moment of silence, he cast his eyes down, like a shy schoolgirl, and declared that he didn't mind telling me that he was a kind of witch, a sâhir, and that he occasionally earned a bit of extra money by casting the odd spell.

It was a while before I could trust myself to speak, partly for fear of laughing, and partly because I knew better than to comment on the impressive range of his skills: I had discovered a while ago that he was very sensitive about what was said about the many little odd jobs he did to earn money—so much so that he had actually fallen ill a few days after we worked out our agreement.

Our paths had first crossed when I was negotiating to rent a set of rooms in an abandoned house, soon after moving to Nashawy. The rooms were part of a house that had been built by the old 'omda, the headman or chief official of the village, a decade or so before the Revolution of 1952. The 'omda was then the largest landowner in the village and the house he built was palatial by local standards, a villa of the kind one might expect to see in the seafront suburbs of Alexandria, with running water, electric lights and toilets. But he died soon after it was completed and the house was locked up and abandoned; his children were successful professionals in Alexandria and Cairo, and they had no interest whatever in their ancestral village. Only one of them even bothered to visit Nashawy any more, a chain-smoking middle-aged woman who occasionally

129

drove down from Alexandria to collect the rent from the few acres that remained with the family after the Revolution. It was she who agreed to let me rent the rooms her father had built for his guests, on the outer side of the main house—a large bedroom with an attached toilet and a little kitchen. The floorboards in the room had long since buckled and warped and the plaster had fallen off the walls, yet the room was comfortable and there was a cheerful feel to it, despite the gloomy shadows of the abandoned house and the eerie rattles it produced at night, when the wind whistled through its unboarded windows and flapping doors.

It was the same woman who had led me to 'Amm Taha: one of his many jobs was that of caretaker. She had suggested that I pay a part of his wages and make an arrangement with him so that he could bring me food cooked by his wife—the kitchen attached to the guest-room was too small for daily use. The matter had been quickly settled and for the first few days after I moved in he arrived at midday, as we had agreed, bringing a few dishes of food with him. But then one afternoon he sent word that he wasn't well, and when he didn't turn up the next day either I decided to go and see what had happened.

His house was in the most crowded part of the village, near the square, where the dwellings were packed so close together that the ricks of straw piled on their roofs almost came together above the narrow, twisting lanes. It was a very small house, a couple of mud-walled rooms with a low, tunnel-like door. 'Amm Taha called out to me to enter when I knocked, but so little light penetrated into the house that it took a while before I could tell where he was.

He was lying on a mat, his thin, crooked face rigid with annoyance, and he began to complain the moment I stepped in:

he was ill, too ill to go anywhere, he didn't know what was going to happen to all his eggs, he had had to send his wife to the market because he hadn't been able to go out for two days.

'But what's happened, ya 'Amm Taha?' I asked. 'Do you know what's wrong?'

His good eye glared angrily at me for a moment, and then he said: 'What do you think has happened? It's the Evil Eye of course—somebody's envied me, what else?'

I looked slowly around the room at the ragged mats and the sooty cooking utensils lying in the corners.

'What did they envy?' I said.

'Can't you see?' he said irritably. 'Everyone's envious of me nowadays. My neighbours see me going to the market every other day, and they say to themselves—that Taha, he has his business in eggs and then he sells milk too, sometimes, as well as vegetables; why, he even has a donkey-cart now, that Taha, and on top of all that, he has so many other little jobs, he's ever so busy all day long, running around making money. What's he going to do with it all? He doesn't even have any children, he doesn't need it.'

He sat up straight and fixed his unmoving eye on me. 'Their envy is burning them up,' he said. 'They're all well-off, but they can't bear to see me working hard and bettering my lot. Over the last few days they've seen me going off to your house, carrying food, and it was just too much for them. They couldn't bear it.'

I began to feel uncomfortable with the part I had been assigned in this narrative: I was not sure whether I was being included amongst the guilty. 'But ya 'Amm Taha,' I said, 'isn't there anything you can do?'

He nodded impatiently; yes, of course, he said, he had already been to the government clinic that morning and they'd given him an injection and some tablets; and now a woman who lived a few doors away was going to come and break the spell—I could stay and watch if I wanted.

The woman arrived a short while later, a plump, talkative matron who seemed more disposed to chatter about the wickedness of their neighbours than to perform her duties. But 'Amm Taha was in a bad temper and he quickly cut her short and handed her a slip of paper, telling her to hurry up if she wanted her fee. She flashed me a smile, and then shutting her eyes she began to stroke his back with the slip of paper, murmuring softly. At times when her voice rose I thought I heard a few phrases of the Fâtiḥa, the opening prayer of the Quran, but for the most part her lips moved soundlessly, without interruption.

After a few minutes of this she opened her eyes and declared plaintively: 'You haven't yawned once, ya 'Amm Taha. You're fine, nobody's envied you.'

This excited a squall of indignation from 'Amm Taha. 'I haven't yawned, did you say?' he snapped. 'How would you know, with your eyes shut?'

'I know you didn't yawn,' she insisted. 'And if you didn't yawn while I was reciting the spell, it means you haven't been envied.'

'Oh is that so? Then look at this,' said 'Amm Taha. Opening his mouth he leaned forward, and when his nose was a bare inch away from hers he produced a gigantic yawn.

She fell back, startled, and began to protest: 'I don't know, ya 'Amm Taha, if you'd really been envied I'd be yawning too. And I haven't yawned at all—can you see me yawning?'

'You're not doing it properly,' he said. 'That's all. Now go on, yalla, try once more.'

She shut her eyes and began to run the slip of paper over his back again, and this time within a few minutes they were both yawning mightily. Soon it was over, and she leant back against the wall, swelling with pride at her success, while 'Amm Taha began to pump his kerosene stove so he could brew us some tea.

'Do you know who it was who envied you?' I asked.

They exchanged a knowing glance, but neither of them would tell me who it was. 'God is the Protector,' 'Amm Taha said piously. 'It doesn't matter who it was—the envy's been undone and I'm fine now.'

The next morning, sure enough, he was back at work, collecting eggs and driving his cart to Damanhour.

Having known of 'Amm Taha's gifts for a while now, I was confident that he would be able to tell me exactly when Ustaz Sabry would be at home.

I was not disappointed.

'Go there this evening,' he said. 'An hour or so after the sunset prayers, and you can be sure you'll find him in.'

5

SURE ENOUGH, USTAZ Sabry was at home when I went to his house that evening: he was sitting in his guest-room surrounded by some half-dozen visitors. He was talking in his clear, powerful voice, holding a shusha in his hands, while the others sat around the room in a circle. A couple of the visitors were dressed in shirts and trousers and looked like college students while the others were fellaheen who had dropped by to spend some time talking at the end of the day.

Ustaz Sabry exclaimed loudly when he saw me at the door, and asked me why I hadn't come earlier, he had been expecting me several days ago. Since his mother had clearly failed to mention my earlier visit, I began to tell him myself, but I had already forfeited Ustaz Sabry's attention: he had launched upon an introduction for the benefit of his visitors.

I was a student from India, he told them, a guest who had come to Egypt to do research. It was their duty to welcome me into their midst and make me feel at home because of the long traditions of friendship between India and Egypt. Our countries were very similar, for India, like Egypt, was largely an agricultural nation, and the majority of its people lived in villages, like the Egyptian fellaheen, and ploughed their land with cattle. Our countries were poor, for they had both been ransacked by imperialists, and now they were both trying, in very similar ways, to cope with poverty and all the other problems that had been bequeathed to them by their troubled histories. It was a difficult task and our two countries had always supported each other in the past: Mahatma Gandhi had come to Egypt to consult Sa'ad Zaghloul Pasha, the leader of the Egyptian nationalist movement, and later Nehru and Nasser had forged a close alliance. No Egyptian could ever forget the support that his country had received from India during the Suez crisis of 1956, when Egypt had been subjected to an unprovoked attack by the British and the French.

One of the men sitting across the room had been shifting impatiently in his seat while Ustaz Sabry made his speech; a small, wizened, prematurely aged man, with a faraway look in his deeply-lined eyes. His name was Zaghloul, I later learnt, and he was a self-taught weaver, who spun his own woollen yarn and wove it on a rudimentary loom.

Now, Zaghloul had a question to ask, and as soon as he found an opportunity he said, in a breathless rush: 'And in his country do they have ghosts like we do?'

'Allah!' Ustaz Sabry exclaimed. 'You could ask him about so many useful and important things—religion or politics—and instead you ask him about ghosts! What will he think of you?'

'I don't know about all that,' Zaghloul said stubbornly. 'What I want to know is whether they have ghosts in his country like we do.'

'What ghosts?' Ustaz Sabry exploded. 'These ghosts you talk about, these 'afârît, they're just products of your own imagination. There are no such things, can't you see? What's the use of asking him about ghosts, what can he tell you? People imagine these things everywhere; in India just as here, there are people who think they see ghosts, and in England and Europe too there are people who point to certain houses and say, "This house is haunted, the ghost of Lord So-and-So walks here at night." But all these things are purely imaginary—no such beings exist.'

'Imaginary!' cried the weaver. 'What do you mean imaginary? How can something be imaginary if someone sees it with his own eyes, right in front of his face?'

'Have you ever seen such a thing?' Ustaz Sabry shot back.

A dreamy look came into the weaver's faraway eyes. 'No,' he said, 'but listen to me, I'll tell you something: my father saw a female ghost once, an 'afrîta, at night as he was walking past the graveyard. He never went that way at night again, by God. Why, and just the other day my neighbour's wife saw a ghost running down the road near the canal, wrapped in a blanket. I can even tell you whose ghost it was; but only if you want to know.'

'Who was it?' someone asked.

'It was Fathy, the Sparrow,' he announced triumphantly. At once, two of the men sitting next to him recoiled in horror, and began to whisper the Fatiha and other protective prayers.

'Do you mean,' I said, 'the man who was killed at the mowlid in Nakhlatain—a few months ago?'

'Yes,' said Zaghloul, 'on God's name, it was him, the Sparrow, who was knocked off a swing and killed at the mowlid. They're saying his ghost has come back to haunt us because his kinsmen were too weak to start a feud or to get the murderer's lineage to pay the proper blood-money.'

At this Ustaz Sabry and one of the college students immediately took issue with him. There was no question of a blood feud, Ustaz Sabry said. The man's death had been proved to be accidental—there had been a police inquiry and the matter had been settled. Feuds and vengeance killings were things of the past; nowadays it was the government's job to deal with crimes and murders.

'The world is wide,' said Zaghloul, 'and with prayers to the Prophet, God have mercy on him, I'll tell you something and you give it mind: something wasn't right about how the whole business of the Sparrow's death was handled. The elders of the killer's family should have gone to the elders of the Sparrow's family, and said to them: Let us sit together and read the Quran and reach an agreement, insha'allah. And while they were sorting things out, the killer should have sought sanctuary somewhere else. But instead there he was, walking freely about, showing no respect for the dead man's rights.'

'But it was an accident,' said Ustaz Sabry. 'The matter went to the police and it was settled, and that was that, khalas.'

'God fortify you, ya Ustaz,' the weaver said, deferential but obstinate. 'You know many things we don't, but something must be wrong, otherwise why is the Sparrow's ghost appearing to so many people?'

Ustaz Sabry clapped his hands to his temples in despair.

'This happens every time,' he said to me. 'Whenever there's an accidental death the talk turns to ghosts and jinns. A few years ago the whole village was gripped by a panic when a boy fell off a roof and died, during the Nashawy mowlid.'

'Does the doktór al-Hindi know about our mowlid?' Zaghloul said eagerly, with a glance in my direction. 'That is a story he should be told.'

Later, when I got to know Zaghloul better, I discovered that besides being very fond of stories, he had a manner of telling them that was marvellously faithful to the metaphorical resonances of his chosen craft. I would often come upon him out in the fields, squatting on his haunches, with his eyes fixed on his hands in an absent, oddly melancholy gaze, spinning yarn, and waiting for someone to talk to. He was, in fact, much better at telling stories than at weaving, for the products of his loom tended to look a bit like sackcloth and never earned him anything more than a generous measure of ridicule. Zaghloul himself had no illusions about the quality of his cloth: he was overcome with shock, for instance, when I asked him to make me a couple of scarves to take back as mementoes. 'You're laughing at me,' he said, 'you want to use my cloth to show your people that the fellaheen of Egypt are backward and primitive.'

His wife was even more astonished than he, especially when she discovered that I intended to pay for the scarves. 'Can't you take him too?' she said, bursting into laughter. 'To show him off to your people?' Later, I discovered that there was a festering bitterness between them that sometimes exploded into ugly quarrels; Zaghloul would threaten to divorce her and marry again, while she retaliated with the taunt—'Do you think anyone would marry you, you shrivelled old man? You're the old man of the village, the 'ajûz al-balad, no one will have you.' It was probably because of these scenes that Zaghloul spent an inordinate amount of time out on the fields, and was always glad to have an audience for his stories.

'The doktór doesn't know the story of Sidi Abu-Kanaka,' Zaghloul announced to the room, and then, leaning back on the divan he took a deep, satisfied puff of his shusha and began at the beginning.

The story was an old one, he said; even when he was a child there were very few people alive who had witnessed the events of that time, and they too had never seen Sidi Abu-Kanaka in the flesh: he had died long before they were born. But everyone knew of him of course, for he had achieved great renown in his lifetime. He was universally mourned when he died and the villagers had even built him a special grave in their cemetery.

Many years later, long after Sidi Abu-Kanaka's death, when the land around Nashawy had become green and thickly populated, the government decided that the time had come to build a canal to serve the farmers of the area. The work began soon enough and the canal proceeded quickly, past Lataifa, all the way down the road, and everyone was glad, for the area had long needed better irrigation. But when the canal reached Nashawy the villagers discovered that a calamity was in the offing, for if it went ahead as the engineers had planned, it would go directly through their cemetery. Everybody was horrified at the thought of disturbing the dead and the elders of the village went to see the government authorities to beg them to change the route. But their complaints only made the effendis impatient; they shut their doors upon the village shaikhs, saying that the canal would have to go on in a straight line, just as it was drawn in the plan.

So the villagers had watched with heavy hearts as the canal ploughed through their graveyard. Then one morning the workmen, to their utter astonishment, came upon a grave that would not yield to their spades; they hammered at it, for days and days, all of them together, but the grave had turned to rock, and no matter how hard they tried they couldn't make the slightest dent in it. When all their efforts failed, the engineers and the big effendis tried to do what they could, but it was to no purpose—they still weren't able to make the least impression on the tomb. At last, realizing that their efforts were in vain, they spoke to the village shaikhs, and upon learning that it was the tomb of Sidi Abu-Kanaka that had thwarted them, they went to his descendants and begged them to open the vault if they could.

'By all means,' the Sidi's grandson said, 'we are at your service,' and at his touch the tomb opened quite easily. Then all the people who had gathered there saw for themselves, what they would never have believed otherwise: that the Sidi's body was still whole and incorrupt, and that instead of being affected by the decay of time, it was giving off a beautiful, perfumed smell.

Everyone who was there was witness to the event and nobody, not even the effendis, could deny the miracle that Sidi Abu-Kanaka had wrought. And so it happened that the canal was made to take a slight diversion there, and on that plot of land the people of the village built a maqâm for the Sidi. The Sidi, in turn, extended his protection over Nashawy and kept its people from harm. Once, for instance, when a gang of armed thieves set out to attack Nashawy the Sidi summoned up a miracle and surrounded the village with a deep, impassable moat. In the years that followed, time and time again, he gave the villagers proof of his benevolence with miracles and acts of grace.

'This is the story that people tell here,' Ustaz Sabry said to me, as I scribbled furiously in my notebook. 'You see how the fellaheen can thwart the government when they choose…'

Yet, although everyone in the village revered the Sidi, there was no mowlid to honour his name; Nashawy's annual mowlid commemorated a saint from the settlement's parent village, far in the interior. Then one year there was a terrible accident at the Nashawy mowlid. A boy who had climbed on to the roof of a house to get a better view of the chanting of the zikr, lost his footing on the straw and fell off, breaking his neck. The people of the village were so horrified that they ran back and shut their doors, and the streets of the village were deserted, night after night, while everyone cowered at home. There were many who interpreted these events as a sign that the village ought to begin celebrating a mowlid in honour of Sidi Abu-Kanaka.

There was so much fear in Nashawy in those days, said Ustaz Sabry, that one night he and some of the other teachers decided that they ought to do something to counter the panic that had overtaken the village. What they did was this: they formed small groups, together with the other educated people in the village, and every night after the sunset prayers they walked through the lanes crying the name of God out loud, and calling upon the fellaheen to come out of their houses. Nobody joined them the first night, but over the next few days more and more people came out, until finally every man was out in the lanes shouting 'Allahu Akbar'. Thus the villagers got over their fear and Nashawy slowly returned to normal.

Later the teachers got together and decided that the time had come to call a halt to the extravagances of the mowlid. The celebration of mowlids for local saints was not a part of the true practice of Islam, Ustaz Sabry argued; such customs only served to encourage superstition and religious laxity. Besides, the fellaheen wasted a lot of money on the mowlid each year, money they had worked hard to earn, and which they would have done better to spend on fertilizers and insecticides.

For a few years after that, the villagers celebrated Sidi Abu-Kanaka's mowlid, but on a much reduced scale. But then there was further disagreement about the saints and their mowlids and in the end the Imam and many others declared that things being as they were, it was better not to hold a mowlid at all.

'Is that Imam Ibrahim you're referring to?' I said.

'Yes,' said Ustaz Sabry, in surprise. 'Have you met him? He hardly goes out at all nowadays.'

'No,' I said, 'I haven't met him. But I've heard a lot about him; people say that he was once famous as a "man of religion" in this area.'

One of the college students, a lean, wiry youth with deep-set eyes, cast a startled glance in my direction. 'Nowadays people laugh at his sermons,' he said. 'He doesn't seem to know about the things that are happening around us, in Afghanistan, Lebanon and Israel.'

Ustaz Sabry shrugged. 'He's from another time,' he said. 'What he knows about religion is what he learnt from his father in the village Qur'an school, the kuttâb.'

'He doesn't know anything about today's world,' said the student. 'When you deliver the Friday sermons, ya Ustaz Sabry, it's so inspiring—everyone feels they should do something about all that's happening in the world around us.'

Ustaz Sabry threw him a nod of acknowledgement. 'It's the times that are different,' he said. 'When Imam Ibrahim was a young man it was very hard for people like him to go to college or university and they didn't have many dealings with the big cities. How were they to learn about the real principles of religion?'

'But I've heard Imam Ibrahim reads a lot,' I said. 'And that he's very knowledgeable about traditional kinds of medicine.'

'Yes,' conceded Ustaz Sabry, 'that is true, no doubt about it. He's read many of the classical texts and he's very knowledgeable about plants and herbs and things like that—or so they say.'

Zaghloul interrupted him with a sudden outburst of laughter. 'Those leaves and powders don't work any more,' he said. 'Nowadays everyone goes to the clinic and gets an injection, and that's the end of it.'

'But Imam Ibrahim's learnt to give injections too,' Ustaz Sabry said, 'just like all the other barbers.'

'Except that he sticks in the needle like it was a spear,' said the weaver.

In the laughter that followed I got up to leave, for it was late now, and I had a long day's notes to write out. Ustaz Sabry rose to see me out and invited me to come back again soon, so we could have another talk. At the door he turned and asked the two college students to accompany me.

'It's dark outside,' he said, overruling my protests. 'You won't be able to find your way back; you city people always get lost in villages. These two boys, Nabeel and Isma'il, will take you to your room.'

6

'I HEARD SOMETHING about those friends of yours,' Shaikh Musa suddenly exclaimed, while we were sitting in his guestroom talking about everything that had happened in the years I had been away. 'You know those two fellows you used to talk about so much, Nabeel and Isma'il—I heard something about them.'

'Yes?' I said. 'What was it?'

'Someone told me, I can't remember who,' he said. 'It was many years after you went back to India.'

He paused to think, scratching his chin while I waited impatiently.

'I heard they were going to Iraq,' he said at last. 'They had gone to Cairo to make the arrangements.'

'Nabeel and Isma'il!' I said. 'Are you sure you're thinking of the right names?'

'Yes,' said Shaikh Musa. 'I would sometimes ask about them when I met people from Nashawy: how they were, what they were doing. Things like that. Didn't you know they were going?'

'No,' I said. I could only shake my head, in stupefaction: it had never occurred to me that Nabeel might have left Egypt and gone abroad.

It was several years now since I had last heard from Nabeel. He and I had corresponded regularly for a while after my departure, but then I had changed address several times in New Delhi, while he had gone off to do his stint in the army, and one way or another our correspondence had been ruptured and never resumed. In the intervening years I had assumed that he and Isma'il had become employees of the Agriculture Ministry, just as they had always intended to.

When I first met them, that night at Ustaz Sabry's house, they were still students at an agricultural training college in Damanhour. They had only a short while to go and once in possession of their degrees they would each be entitled to a job in the Agriculture Ministry. They knew it would be several years before they actually got those jobs—they would have to serve their drafts in the army first, and then there would be a long wait while the Ministry tried to find places for them (no easy matter since it had to cope with thousands of new graduates every year). Still they were very sure in their minds that the eventual security would be well worth the wait, and they had both decided long before that they would send their papers in to the Ministry as soon as they had served their time in the army.

It was no coincidence that their visions of the future were so similar: they were best friends as well as cousins; their mothers were sisters, strong-willed, resourceful women who had always told their children that only by hanging closely together would their families be able to make their way in a harsh and hostile world.

They had both hoped that they would be sent to Nashawy or some other village co-operative nearby once they got their jobs in the Agriculture Ministry. In Nashawy, as in the rest of Egypt, landowning farmers had been organized into a co-operative soon after the Revolution of 1952. The co-op was staffed by a small complement of Agriculture Ministry employees, who advised the fellaheen on technical matters. These officers were a significant force in the village, almost as much so as the schoolteachers, for although their profession lacked the moral authority that went with teaching, it gave them much more real power: it was they, for instance, who dealt with the vitally important (and potentially lucrative) business of distributing government-subsidized fertilizers and insecticides.

In general the officers of the co-operative preferred to exercise their powers from a magisterial distance: they held themselves apart from the fellaheen, and would consort with no one in the village except a few schoolteachers. Inevitably their aloofness lent them a certain glamour in the villagers' eyes: schoolboys kept a close eye on their styles of dress, ambitious mothers subtly courted the bachelors amongst them, and everyone except the teachers deferred to their views on subjects such as politics and religion.

Like many of their peers, Nabeel and Isma'il had wanted to become officers in the Nashawy co-op ever since their boyhood. They usually spoke of that ambition in terms of convenience: of how they would save money by living at home, how they would be able to help their families and look after their parents, how their mothers wanted them to be in the village so they could start thinking of suitable marriages and so on. But behind that matter-of-fact reasoning there was a rich and glossy backdrop of remembered images: memories from a time when they had gathered around the doors of the co-op and eavesdropped on the officers, talking about the great world outside, until they were chased away with yells—'Get going you kids, you sons of bitches, get out of here.' Over the years, it had become their dearest ambition to see themselves installed behind those very desks.

'I think Nabeel and Isma'il left for Iraq soon after they did their draft,' Shaikh Musa said. 'I thought they would have written to you.'

He shook his head, smiling. 'They were fine young fellows, real jad'ân,' he said. 'I only heard good things about them;

everyone always spoke well of those two.'

But Shaikh Musa had taken a different view at first. He had been shocked to hear that Isma'il had spoken dismissively of Imam Ibrahim. 'Those students!' he had exclaimed indignantly. 'They think they know everything.' It was hard for him to accept that the public life of the area had changed almost beyond recognition since his own youth.

For Isma'il it was Ustaz Sabry who was a figure of respect, not Imam Ibrahim: he talked of him at length when he and Nabeel accompanied me back to my room that night when I first met them. There was no one in the village he admired more, he said; no one from whom he had learned as much, nobody he so dearly wished to emulate. It was Ustaz Sabry, for instance, who had first thought of raising money for the Afghans: in a speech at the mosque, he had talked of how Muslims were being slaughtered by Communists in Afghanistan, and the men of the village were so moved they raised quite an impressive sum of money for the mujahideen. On another occasion, in a speech on superstitions and mistaken beliefs he had eloquently condemned the custom that women observed, of leaving offerings at the graves of dead relatives. He had described the practice as unlawful and contrary to the spirit of Islam, and his speech was so powerful and convincing that the men went straight home from the mosque, and forbade the womenfolk to do it again. He and the other teachers had even succeeded in uniting the villagers against a man who was known to perform exorcism rituals for women, secret Ethiopian rites called Zâr: a large group of men had gone to confront him and they had told him to put an end to his doings.

When Ustaz Sabry put his mind to it, said Isma'il, he could always prevail upon others, because no one was more skilled in disputation than he. Friends who had served in the army with him told a story about an argument he had once had with an East German, a Communist military expert who was attached to their unit. The German had been in Egypt many years and spoke Arabic well.

'Do you believe in God?' the German had asked, and when Ustaz Sabry answered yes, he certainly did, the German replied: 'So then where is he, show me?'

Ustaz Sabry countered by asking him a question in turn. 'Tell me,' he said, 'do you believe that people have a spirit, the spirit of life itself?'

'Yes,' the German answered, so then Ustaz Sabry said to him: 'Where is this spirit, can you show it to me?'

'It is in no one place' the German replied, 'it is everywhere— in the body, the head…'

'And that,' Ustaz Sabry said, 'is exactly where God is.'

The German knew he was beaten, but he wasn't willing to admit defeat. 'I don't believe in God,' he insisted, 'we Communists think of religion as the opium of the masses.'

'You can believe what you please,' Ustaz Sabry had told him, 'but you will see that the people of your own country will soon sicken of your atheistic beliefs, just as we have in Egypt.'

It was a story that was often repeated.

Ustaz Sabry and the other young teachers had completely changed Nashawy, said Isma'il; they were constantly active, constantly battling against ignorance. Now they had even hatched a plan to start a consumers' co-operative that would sell essentials like rice, sugar, oil and suchlike at rock-bottom prices, so that the people of Nashawy would no longer have to put up with the sinful profiteering of the village's shopkeepers. In time, with the help of God, they would succeed in rooting out all exploitation and unbelief from the village, and people would see for themselves where the path of true Islam lay.

Nabeel had said very little while Isma'il was talking, apart from murmuring a few noises of assent. Later I discovered that this was not unusual: Isma'il usually did the talking when the two of them were together. There was a kind of complementarity between them, a close-stitched seam of differences which became ever more visible when they were in each other's company. Nabeel was the quiet, reflective one, not shy, but serious and earnest, never saying anything or committing himself without a good deal of prior thought. Isma'il, on the other hand, was like a bird—or so his family said—giving voice to every passing thought and always ready with a joke or a pun. You could see the difference between them from a long way off: Nabeel was stocky, with a square, tidy face, while Isma'il was short, wiry and aquiline; when Nabeel walked through the village it was with a steady, considered kind of gait, but Isma'il, in contrast, walked with quick, jaunty steps, and always seemed to be in a hurry to get where he was going.

When I came to know the cousins better, I understood that the differences between them were no less a product of their upbringing than the ties that held them together: it was true that their mothers were sisters, and very alike in many ways, but their fathers were quite unlike one another, and the difference in their characters had left a profound mark on the children. Isma'il's father belonged to a humble lineage of small tradesmen, but he was a hard-working, cheerful man, a good provider who had succeeded in handing on something of his own optimistic spirit to his children. Nabeel's father, Idris, on the other hand, was a member of the largest and most powerful lineage in the village, the Badawy. But, of course, not all the

Badawy were alike in their material circumstances, and it so happened that Idris belonged to one of the clan's most impoverished branches. He himself had almost nothing in the world apart from the house he and his family lived in, a dilapidated complex of three mud-walled rooms grouped around a tiny courtyard. His forefathers had owned a fair bit of land once, but they had somehow contrived to lose it, and ever since, their descendants had been forced to make their living in the lowliest possible way, by working as labourers on other people's land, for daily wages.

Idris had been presented with a rare opportunity to improve his circumstances when he was allotted some land after the Revolution of 1952. But at about that time, quite by chance, he also managed to find employment as a village watchman, a post that carried a monthly salary. To his way of thinking, it was infinitely more respectable to be a mowazzaf, a 'salaried employee', than a fellah, sweating in the mud, so he decided to take the watchman's job. It would have been hard for him to work the land anyway, he had reasoned, because his oldest son was just an infant then, and he wasn't strong enough to farm a couple of feddans on his own. So he let the land go, and over the following years, eking out an existence on his watchman's salary, he had watched regretfully while the other recipients of Reform land slowly gained in prosperity and built themselves bigger and better houses.

Yet Idris bore no grudges and counted it an achievement that he had succeeded in becoming a mowazzaf even if his job was a humble one and his wages negligible. Once, he showed me the gun he had been issued in his capacity as a watchman: he was hugely proud of it and kept it locked in a trunk under his bed. It was a British-made Enfield, of considerable antiquity, not far removed from a blunderbuss in fact. When he stood it on the floor it looked like an up-ended cannon, reaching higher than his shoulder and dwarfing him, with his frail, stooped frame and his tendril-thin wrists. I had difficulty in believing that he had ever been able to raise that redoubtable weapon to his chin, much less fire it, but he assured me I was wrong, that he had indeed used it on several occasions in the past. The last time admittedly was some fifteen years ago, when he let fly at some thieves who were escaping through a cornfield: the thieves got away but a large patch of corn was flattened by the blast.

Idris was not personally unhappy with his lot for he counted it an honour to be paid a monthly salary by the government. Nabeel, on the other hand, hated his family's poverty, and loyal though he was to his father, he considered a watchman's job demeaning, unworthy of his lineage. He had always been treated as a poor relative by his more prosperous Badawy cousins, and he had responded by withdrawing into the defensive stillness of introspection. But there was a proud streak in him and, even more than Isma'il, he was determined to escape his poverty and improve his family's condition.

Fortunately for Nabeel, his mother, through a mixture of determination and good sense, had succeeded in providing him and his younger brothers with the necessary means for bettering their lot. She had taken her oldest son, 'Ali, out of school at an early age, and sent him out to work in the fields. Realizing that her family's best hope lay in educating the other children, she had somehow contrived to keep the family going, with the help of 'Ali's meagre earnings, while Nabeel and his younger brothers went through school and college. But she was acutely aware all along that it was 'Ali's sacrifice that had given the others the possibility of a better future, and to show her gratitude, she set about arranging his marriage as soon as it became clear that, God willing, nothing could now prevent Nabeel from graduating.

Nabeel and Isma'il told me about 'Ali's forthcoming wedding at our very first meeting, when they walked with me from Ustaz Sabry's house to my room. I asked them in when we reached my door, and while I made tea Isma'il talked at length about the forthcoming wedding.

'Ali was going to marry Isma'il's sister, Fawzia (who was, of course, his first cousin)—now, apart from being best friends and cousins, he and Nabeel would also be linked by marriage! It was the best kind of union, he said: the bride and groom were cousins and had known each other all their lives; they were of the same age and they had virtually lived in each other's houses since the day they were born. There would be no outsiders involved, everything would be kept within the family and arranged between relatives, so there would be none of those problems that went with bringing a stranger into one's household.

'We will sing and dance for the bride and groom,' said Isma'il. 'You must come: it will be a sight that you will remember.'

'I shall be honoured to come,' I said. 'It will be a privilege.'

Nabeel in the meanwhile had been running his eyes silently around my room, looking from my clothes, hanging on pegs, to my paper-strewn desk and the pots and pans stored in the tiny space that served as a makeshift kitchen. He seemed to become wholly absorbed in his scrutiny while Isma'il talked and I busied myself with the tea; he looked at everything in turn with a deep and preoccupied concentration, running his hands over his jallabeyya.

Suddenly, as I was spooning tea into my kettle, he spoke up, interrupting Isma'il.

'It must make you think of all the people you left at home,' he said to me, 'when you put that kettle on the stove with just enough water for yourself.'

There was a brief pause and then Isma'il said quickly: 'Why should it? He has us and so many other friends to come here and have tea with him; he has no reason to be lonely.'

'It's not the same thing,' said Nabeel. 'Think how you would feel.'

The conversation quickly turned to something else, but Nabeel's comment stayed in my mind; I was never able to forget it, for it was the first time that anyone in Lataifa or Nashawy had attempted an enterprise similar to mine—to enter my imagination and look at my situation as it might appear to me.

It took me some time to absorb the fact that Nabeel and Isma'il were gone now: for a while I found it hard to believe what Shaikh Musa had told me. In the many years that had passed since I last met them, I had grown accustomed to thinking of the two cousins as officers in the co-op; I had even tried to imagine what their responses would be when I walked through the door.

'Nabeel came with me to the station the day I left Nashawy,' I told Shaikh Musa. 'He said that by the time I returned he would have his job and be settled in Nashawy.'

'Do you know why they left?' I asked. 'Was there any specific reason?'

Shaikh Musa shrugged. 'Why does anyone leave?' he said. 'The opportunity comes, and it has to be taken.'

7

To THE YOUNG Ben Yiju, journeying eastwards would have appeared as the simplest and most natural means of availing himself of the most rewarding possibilities his world had to offer.

His own origins lay in Ifriqiya—in the Mediterranean port of Mahdia, now a large town in Tunisia. His family name 'ibn Yijû'—or Ben Yijû, in Hebrew—was probably derived from the name of a Berber tribe that had once been the protectors, or patrons, of his lineage. The chronology of his childhood and early life is hazy, and nothing is known exactly about the date or place of his birth. Working backwards from the events of his later life, it would seem that the date of his birth was somewhere towards the turn of the century, in the last years of the eleventh or the first of the twelfth. Since his friends sometimes referred to him as 'al-Mahdawî' it seems likely that he was born in Mahdia, which was then a major centre of Jewish culture, as well as one of the most important ports in Ifriqiya.

A contemporary of Ben Yiju's, the Sharîf al-Idrîsî, a distinguished Arab geographer, developed a personal acquaintance with Mahdia at about the time that Ben Yiju would have been growing up there. He had a few sharp words to say about the quality of its water, but otherwise he found much to admire in the town: it had pretty buildings, nice promenades, magnificent baths, and numerous caravanserais; its inhabitants were generally good-looking and well-dressed and 'altogether Mahdia offered a view of something wonderful'.

Of Ben Yiju's immediate family, only two brothers, Yûsuf and Mubashshir, and one sister, Berâkhâ, figure in his later correspondence. Nothing at all is known about his mother, and very little about his father, apart from his name and a few incidental details. He was called Peraḥyâ (spelt Farḥîa in Arabic), and he was a Rabbi, a respected scholar and scribe. He may have dabbled in business, like most scholars of his time, but the family's circumstances seem to have been modest, and in all likelihood his principal bequest to his sons lay in the excellent education he provided them with.

Abraham Ben Yiju was certainly well enough educated to have become a scholar himself and he was very well versed in doctrinal and religious matters. His personal inclinations, however, appear to have tended towards the literary rather than the scholastic: he was an occasional poet, and he wrote a clear, carefully crafted prose, with some arresting images hidden under a deceptively plain surface.

But for all that, when it came to a choice of career the opportunities offered by the eastern trade must have seemed irresistible to the young Ben Yiju, reared as he was in a community that had made a speciality of it. And once he had launched upon it, that career would have followed a natural progression, leading him from Ifriqiya to Fustat, and then to Aden, the port that sat astride the most important sea-routes connecting the Middle East and the Indian Ocean.

Ben Yiju's papers leave no room for doubt that he did indeed move to Aden, probably for a considerable length of time, in the 1120s, or maybe even earlier. The exact dates and duration of his stay may never be known, however, because not a single scrap of material dating from that period of his life has survived: apart from a few pinpricks of light, refracted back from the letters he received in India, those years are shrouded in dark obscurity.

However, it is clear enough from his later correspondence that his early years in Aden played a formative part in his life. It was probably there, for example, that he made the acquaintance of a man who was to become first his mentor and then his partner in business, a wealthy and powerful trader called Maḍmûn ibn al-Ḥasan ibn Bundâr.

Madmun ibn Bundar, like his father before him, was the Nagîd or Chief Representative of merchants, in Aden. He was thus the head of the city's large and wealthy Jewish community, as well as the superintendent of the port's customs offices—a man of great substance and influence, a key figure in the Indian Ocean trade, whose network of friends and acquaintances extended all the way from Spain to India.

Several of Madmun's letters figure in Ben Yiju's correspondence: crisp and straightforward in style, they are written in the prose of a bluff, harried trader, with no frills, and many fewer wasted words than was usual at the time. The letters are often spread over a number of different folio sheets, some written in his own hand, and some by scribes. Madmun himself wrote a terrible hand, a busy, trader's scrawl, forged in the bustle of the market-place. Often the carefully calligraphed copies produced by his team of scribes end in swathes of his own hasty handwriting: there is a freshness and urgency about them which make it all too easy to see him snatching the letters away to add a few final instructions while the ships that are to carry them wait in the harbour below.

Ben Yiju almost certainly knew of Madmun long before he left Egypt, and his friends and relatives are sure to have armed him with letters of introduction when he set out for Aden. Madmun, for his part, had probably been warned of the newcomer's impending arrival by his own networks of information, and he may well have been favourably disposed towards him even before he reached Aden. For a young man in Ben Yiju's circumstances there could have been no more fortunate connection than to have the Chief Representative of Merchants as his patron: fortunately for him he appears to have made a favourable impression on Madmun, and it was probably in his warehouse that he first learned the rudiments of the Indian Ocean trade.

Madmun's earliest extant letters date from after Ben Yiju's departure from Aden, when he was engaged in setting up in business in the Malabar. From the tone and content of those early letters it would seem that Ben Yiju's relationship with Madmun at that time fell somewhere between that of an agent and a junior partner. The letters are full of detailed instructions, and beneath the surface of their conventionally courteous language there is a certain peremptoriness, as though Madmun were doubtful of the abilities and efficiency of his inexperienced associate. But at the same time it is amply clear from Madmun's warm but occasionally irascible tone that he regarded Ben Yiju with an almost parental affection. His familiarity with his tastes and habits suggests that he may even have taken the young Ben Yiju to live in his household, regarding him as a part of his family, in much the same way that artisans sometimes made their apprentices their presumptive kin.

Indeed, Ben Yiju appears to have been warmly welcomed by the whole of Madmun's close-knit social circle in Aden. His two other principal correspondents there were both related to Madmun. One of them, Yûsuf ibn Abraham, was a judicial functionary as well as a trader: a man of a somewhat self-absorbed and irritable disposition, on the evidence of his letters. The other was Khalaf ibn Ishaq—the writer of the letter of MS

H.6, and possibly the closest of Ben Yiju's friends in Aden.

The fortunes of each of these men were founded on the trade between India and the Middle East but their part in it was that of brokers and financiers rather than travelling merchants. At one time or another they too had probably travelled extensively in the Indian Ocean, but by the time Ben Yiju met them they were all comfortably settled in Aden, with their days of travel behind them.

There was no lack of travellers in their circle, however: at least two of Madmun's friends deserve to be counted amongst the most well-travelled men of the Middle Ages, perhaps of any age before the twentieth century. The first was a prominent figure in the Jewish community of Fustat, Abû Sa'îd Ḥalfon ben Nethan'el ha-Levi al-Dimyâṭî, a wealthy merchant, scholar and patron of literature, whose surname links him to the Egyptian port of Dumyâṭ or Damietta. A large number of Abu Sa'id Halfon's papers have been preserved in the Geniza and their dates and places of writing bear witness to a pattern of movement so fluent and far-ranging that they make the journeys of later medieval travellers, such as Marco Polo and Ibn Battuta, seem unremarkable in comparison. From year to year he was resident in different countries and continents, travelling frequently between Egypt, India, East Africa, Syria, Morocco and Spain. He was also a close friend and patron of one of the greatest of medieval Hebrew poets, Judah ha-Levi, who dedicated a treatise to him and composed a number of poems in his honour. Abu Sa'id Halfon regularly corresponded and did business with Madmun and Khalaf, and although there is no record of a direct exchange of letters between him and Ben Yiju, there can be no doubt that they were well acquainted with each other.

The second of the great travellers of Madmun's circle was

Abû-Zikrî Judah ha-Kohen Sijilmâsî. As his name suggests, Abu Zikri Sijilmasi had his origins in the desert town of Sijilmasa in Morocco, but he later emigrated to Fustat and rose to prominence within the Jewish community there, eventually becoming the Chief Representative of Merchants. He too travelled far afield, between Egypt, Aden, southern Europe and India. References in Ben Yiju's correspondence show that he frequently encountered Abu Zikri Sijilmasi and his brother-in-law, a ship-owner called Maḥrûz, in Mangalore. So close were the links between the three of them that on one occasion, when Abu Zikri Sijilmasi was captured by pirates off the coast of Gujarat, Ben Yiju penned him a letter on behalf of Mahruz, urging him to travel quickly down from Broach to Mangalore.

It was probably no coincidence, since merchant families have always tightened the bonds of trade with a tug of kinship, that Abu Zikri's Sijilmasi's sister happened to be married to Madmun. It could well be that it was Abu Zikri who, out of allegiance to a fellow North African, gave Ben Yiju the introduction which secured his entry into Madmun's circle.

Circumstances were thus propitious for Ben Yiju's introduction into Madmun's privileged circle in Aden. Still, it needs to be noted that if Ben Yiju succeeded in finding ready acceptance within the society of the wealthy merchants of Aden, despite his comparatively humble standing as a young apprentice trader, it must have been largely because of his individual gifts. His distinction of mind is evident enough in his letters, but he must have had, in addition, a certain warmth or charm, as well as the gift of inspiring loyalty—qualities whose attribution is none the more doubtful for being a matter of conjecture since their indisputable proof lies in the long friendships enshrined in his correspondence.

The circle which the young Ben Yiju was received into in Aden was one that had place for literary talent as well as business acumen. At the time of his stay there were several gifted Hebrew poets living and writing in Aden. It was an ambience that must have been attractive in the extreme to a man of Ben Yiju's tastes, with his inclination for poetry and his diligence in business. That, combined with the warmth of his welcome into an exclusive society, must have made Aden an extraordinarily congenial place for this young trader with a literary bent.

Yet, curiously enough, at some point before 1132 Ben Yiju moved to the Malabar coast and did not return to Aden for nearly two decades.

At first glance there appears to be nothing unusual about Ben Yiju's departure, for of course, merchants involved in the eastern trade travelled frequently to India. But there are two good reasons why this particular move appears anomalous, a deviation from the usual pattern of traders' travels.

The first is that merchants involved in the eastern trade, like Abu Saʿid Halfon and Abu Zikri Sijilmasi for example, generally travelled back and forth at regular intervals between the ports of the Indian Ocean and the Middle East. While there are a few other instances in the Geniza of traders living abroad for long periods of time, none of them quite matches the continuous duration of Ben Yiju's stay—he does not seem to have travelled back to Aden or Egypt even once in the nineteen or twenty years that he was in India. Indeed, it would seem that when the need arose he preferred to send his slave—the slave of MS H.6—to Aden to transact his business there, while he himself remained in Mangalore.

The second reason for suspecting that there may have been

something out of the ordinary in Ben Yiju's departure from Aden
lies in a cryptic letter that is now in the possession of the Taylor-
Schechter collection in Cambridge. This particular piece of paper
is quite large, about eleven inches long and more than five inches
wide, but it is still only a fragment—a scrap which Ben Yiju tore
from a longer sheet so he could scribble on its back. The little
that remains of the original letter is badly damaged and much of
the text is difficult to decipher. Fortunately the scrap does
contain the name of the letter's sender: it is just barely legible and
it serves to link the fragment with this story for it proves that the
writer was none other than Madmun ibn al-Hasan ibn Bundar,
of Aden.

For most of its length, the letter is perfectly straightforward:
following the conventional protocols of their correspondence
Madmun refers to Ben Yiju as 'my master' and to himself as his
'servant'. He begins by acknowledging a shipment of areca nuts,
mentions the sale of a quantity of pepper, and lets Ben Yiju
know that certain goods have been safely delivered to his two
other associates in Aden.

The puzzling part of the letter comes towards the end, and it
consists of a short, six-line passage. It reads thus:

'Concerning what he [my master] mentioned [in his letter]:
that he has resolved to return to Aden, but that which prevents
him [from returning] is the fear that it would be said that he had
acted rashly. His servant spoke to [the king] al-Mâlik al-Sa'îd
concerning him...and took from him his guarantee as a
safeguard against his return, insha'allah. So he [my master] has
nothing to fear: [the king] will resolve everything in his court in
the country of India. And if, God forfend, he were to lose...what
he has and his children were part of that [loss]...'

The rest is lost; it was upon this tantalizingly incomplete line that Ben Yiju's hands fell when he was tearing up the letter. No other document contains any mention of whatever matter it was that Madmun was referring to in his letter: unless the rest of the letter is discovered some day nothing more will ever be known of it.

Despite its brevity and the suddenness of its termination, there is one fact the passage does serve to establish beyond any doubt. It proves that Ben Yiju's departure for India was not entirely voluntary—that something had happened in Aden that made it difficult for him to remain there or to return.

The passage provides no direct indication of what it was that had happened. The most obvious possibility is that the matter had to do with a debt or a financial irregularity. But on the other hand, it is hardly likely that the ruler of Aden would take an interest in a purely civil dispute, as the letter suggests. In any case, if it were only an unpaid debt that prevented Ben Yiju's return to Aden, he and his friends would surely have settled the matter quickly and quietly, without recourse to the ruler.

The passage, such as it is, provides little enough to go on, and the careful discretion of Madmun's language has wound a further sheet of puzzles around an affair that is already shrouded in mystery. For instance, the word Madmun uses to describe the safeguard offered by the ruler of Aden is one of those Arabic terms that can spin out a giddying spiral of meanings. The word is dhimma, whose parent and sister words mean both 'to blame' as well as the safeguards that can be extended to protect the blameworthy.

Used as it is here, the word could mean that the ruler of Aden had agreed not to prosecute Ben Yiju for a crime that he had committed, or been accused of. Or it could mean that he had pledged to protect him from certain people whose enmity Ben

Yiju had cause to fear. By Arab tradition this was the kind of guarantee that was extended to a man who had killed someone: it was intended to protect him and his relatives from a vengeance killing so that they could raise the murdered man's blood-money.

That implicit suggestion, along with the hint that the matter somehow implicated Ben Yiju's children as well as himself, is all there is to suggest that Ben Yiju may have fled to India in order to escape a blood feud.

For all we know, it could just as well have been a matter of unpaid taxes.

8

SHAIKH MUSA HAD never heard of Khamees the Rat before I mentioned his name.

He pursed his lips when I asked him, and began to finger his beads, thinking hard, but after a while, loath to admit defeat, he gave a peremptory shake of his head and exclaimed: 'The Rat? Al-Fâr? What sort of name is that? Are you sure you heard it right?'

It was a nickname, I said, his relations called him that because of the way he talked, because he gnawed at things with his tongue like a rat did with its teeth.

But in fact I didn't really know how he had got the name: for all I knew it could have been his appearance that bestowed it upon him. It was easy to imagine his thin face and bright, darting eyes putting his cousins in mind of a rodent, years ago, when he was a boy; even now, in his mid-twenties with two marriages behind him, something of that resemblance still remained, a certain quickness of movement and a ferile, beady-eyed wit.

'His land is near Zaghloul the weaver's,' I added, for it was often details like that which helped Shaikh Musa make connections. But this time, despite his best efforts, the name eluded the tripwires of his memory.

'Nashawy is a big place,' he said at last, philosophically. 'Which family are they from, do you know?'

The Jammâl, I said, and when I saw the faint curl that came upon his lips it struck me suddenly that of course, that was the reason why Shaikh Musa did not know Khamees—his lineage. People like the Latifs and the Badawy tended to look down their noses at the Jammal; they were unmannerly in their ways, the Badawy would whisper, uncouth in behaviour and wild in temperament, and it was best to keep them at a distance. But they were always careful to lower their voices when they said those things: the Jammal were both very numerous and very pugnacious, and everyone knew that their men would be out in the lanes at the least provocation, eager to fight for their honour.

It stuck in the throats of Nabeel and his Badawy kin that the Jammal had been the biggest gainers from the redistribution of land that had followed the Revolution of 1952: their hostility was now spiced with envy, because from being the poorest people in the village, mere labourers and sharecroppers, many of the Jammal had gone on to become landowning fellaheen, with several feddans of land to their name. Now the Badawy could no longer afford to be so haughty as they once were, and when they received a proposal of marriage from one of the more prosperous Jammal families, they were often all too quick to accept. But still, for people like Shaikh Musa the majority of the Jammal still fell outside the boundaries of respectability, despite the dramatic changes of the last few decades.

Suddenly I recalled another, more promising detail, one that was sure to sound an echo in Shaikh Musa's memory. 'You may know Khamees's sister,' I said. 'She was married not far from you, in Nakhlatain, but she left her husband a few months ago and moved back to Nashawy with her children.'

'Oh my eyes!' Shaikh Musa cried. 'The tall sweet-looking one, who had two little boys—is that the woman you mean?'

Yes, I said, exactly. That was her, tall and sweet-looking; her name was Busaina and she was Khamees's sister.

It was thanks to 'Amm Taha that I knew those details about her: if it were not for him, the self-contained world of Nashawy's women would have been even more firmly closed for me than it was for other men, since unlike them, I had no female relatives in the village to keep me abreast of that parallel history.

I had asked 'Amm Taha about Busaina the very first day I met her, out in the fields during the rice harvest, with Khamees and the rest of her family. I hadn't even known who she was then, for only the mens' names were mentioned, as always. But while we were talking, someone had pointed to the child in her arms and announced with a laugh that there was Khamees's son. As far as I knew no one joked about things like that, so naturally I had concluded that they were married.

'Amm Taha had corrected me the moment I described her. No, he had explained, with his dry, coughing laugh; that wasn't Khamees's wife I had seen, it couldn't have been if she were holding a baby because Khamees didn't have any children. He had been married off at the age of fifteen, several years ago, and having failed to father any children, he had taken a second wife recently, but with no result. The marriage had caused quite a scandal because his first wife had walked off in a rage, shouting to the world that it was his fault that he was childless, not hers. And after all that trouble, the marriage had made no difference —several of Khamees's brothers had families now, but despite being the oldest and the longest married, he remained without child, and was often the butt of their jokes.

'So that couldn't have been his wife you saw,' 'Amm Taha said, wagging a finger in my direction. 'That was probably his sister, Busaina, who's just come back to Nashawy with her children.'

Busaina had been married off years ago to a man from Nakhlatain, not far from Lataifa. But although she had given her husband two fine, healthy children, the two of them had never really got on. They had quarrelled all the time, over this and that, and in the end things had come to such a pass that her husband had announced that he was going to marry again. She told him plainly at the time that she'd leave him if he did, and sure enough, when she heard rumours that he'd been talking with another girl's father, she picked up her things, her pots, pans and furniture, and moved back to Nashawy with her children. So now she was back in her father's house, along with Khamees and all her other brothers and their children.

'It was bound to happen,' Shaikh Musa said. 'She wouldn't listen to anyone. She and her husband used to quarrel all day long because she had to have her way in everything.'

He shook his head ruefully, running a hand over his white-stubbled chin.

'It was because of her origins,' he said. 'The Jammal are all like that, difficult and quarrelsome, and it's best to keep them at a distance.'

He did not look at me, but there was an air of disapproval about him that warned me not to tell him about my first meeting with Khamees and his family.

It was Zaghloul the weaver who had made the introductions. It was the time of the rice harvest, late autumn, and he had spotted me walking through the fields, notebook in hand, and had shouted across: 'Come here, ya doktór—come and eat with us, over here.'

He was sitting with a group of people on a tree-shaded knoll which served to house a couple of wooden water-wheels. He, and the other men in the group were seated cross-legged around a huge tin tray; I could tell from the number of dishes in front of them that they were eating a generous midday meal of the kind that always accompanied a harvest. The women who had brought the food out to the fields were squatting beside them, doling out servings of rice, cheese, salâṭa and fish.

One woman had withdrawn a little from the rest of the group; she was sitting apart, leaning against a tree, with a scarf thrown carelessly over her shoulders, holding a baby to her breast. She looked up as I made my way across the newly-harvested rice fields, fixing me with a clear, inquiring gaze, and when the scarf slipped inadvertently off her breast she straightened it without the slightest show of confusion or shyness. She had a wide, oval face, with well-defined features, and eyes that were brilliantly forthright and direct.

When I reached the knoll Zaghloul stretched out a hand to me, laughing uproariously. 'These men were scared when they saw you walking down the path,' he said, 'because of that notebook in your hands. They thought you were an effendi from Damanhour who'd come to check whether anyone's evading military service.'

He cast a glance at the sheepish grins on the faces around him, his small wizened face crumpling up with mirth.

'So I told them,' he said, 'why no, that's not a military inspector; he's not an effendi or even a veterinarian—that's the doktór from al-Hind, where they have ghosts just like we do.'

'Ahlan!' said the man sitting next to him, a sharp-faced young fellah in a brown jallabeyya. 'Ahlan! So you're the doktór from al-Hind?'

'Yes,' I said, 'and you?'

'He's a rat,' someone answered, raising a gale of laughter. 'Don't go anywhere near him.'

His name was Khamees, said Zaghloul, laughing louder than the rest, Khamees the Rat, and the others sitting there were his brothers and cousins. Their land ran next to each others', he explained, so they always worked together as a group. It was Khamees's family's land they were working on today; it would be his own tomorrow and so on, until they all finished harvesting their rice, in one short week of hard work and good eating.

'Why are you still standing, ya doktór?' cried Khamees. 'You've come a long way and you won't be able to get back to your country before sundown anyway, so you may as well sit with us for a while.'

He moved up, smiling, and slapped the earth beside him. He was in his mid-twenties, about my age, scrawny, with a thin mobile face, deeply scorched by the sun. Almost in spite of myself, I felt instantly at home with him: he had that brightness of eye and the slightly sardonic turn to his mouth that I associated with coffee-houses in Delhi and Calcutta; he seemed to belong to a familiar world of lecture-rooms, late-night rehearsals and black coffee.

He leant back to look at me now, as I seated myself, summing me up with his sharp, satirical eyes.

'All right, ya doktór,' he said, once I had settled in beside him with my legs crossed. 'Tell me, is it true what they say, that in your country you burn your dead?'

The moment he said it the women in the group clasped their hands to their hearts and cried in breathless horror: 'Ḥarâm! Ḥarâm!' and several of the men began to mutter prayers, calling upon the Lord to protect them from the devil.

My heart sank: this was a question I encountered almost daily, and since I had not succeeded in finding a word such as 'cremate' in Arabic, I knew I would have to give my assent to the term that Khamees had used: the verb 'to burn', which was the word for what happened to firewood and straw and the eternally damned.

'Yes,' I said, knowing that I would not be able to prevent the inevitable outcome. 'Yes, it's true; some people in my country burn their dead.'

'You mean,' said Khamees in mock horror, 'that you put them on heaps of firewood and just light them up?'

'Yes,' I said quickly, hoping he would tire of the subject.

It was not to be. 'Why?' he persisted. 'Is there a shortage of kindling in your country?'

'No,' I said, 'you don't understand.'

There was a special word, I tried to explain, a special ceremony, certain rites and rituals—it wasn't like lighting a bonfire with a matchstick. But for all the impression my explanation made, I may as well have been silent.

'Even little children?' said Khamees. 'Do you burn little children?'

Busaina spoke now, for the first time. 'Of course not,' she said, in disbelief, hugging her baby to her breast. 'They wouldn't burn little dead children—no one could do that.'

'Yes,' I said, regretfully. 'Yes, we do—we burn everyone.'

'But why?' she cried. 'Why? Are people fish that you should fry them on a fire?'

'I don't know why,' I said. 'It's the custom—that's how it was when I came into the world. I had nothing to do with it.'

'There's nothing to be surprised at, really,' Zaghloul said wisely, gazing at the horizon. 'Why, in the land of Nam-Nam people even eat their dead. My uncle told me: it's their custom—they can't help it.'

'Stop jabbering, ya Zaghloul,' Busaina snapped at him, and then turned her attention back to me.

'You must put an end to this burning business,' she said to me firmly. 'When you go back you should tell them about our ways and how we do these things.'

'I will,' I promised, 'but I don't know if they'll listen. They're very stubborn, they go on doing the same thing year after year.'

Suddenly Khamees clapped his hands with an exultant cry. 'I'll tell you why they do it,' he said. 'They do it so their bodies can't be punished upon the Day of Judgement.'

The others keeled over with laughter while he looked around in triumph, his eyes astart with the thrill of discovery. 'Don't you see?' he said. 'It's really clever—they burn the bodies so there'll be nothing left to punish and they won't have to answer for their sins.'

'No, no, that's not true,' I said, obscurely offended by this imputation. But no sooner had I begun to argue than I realized that Khamees's interpretation was not intended as a slur: on the contrary he was overcome by a kind of appalled admiration at the wiliness of 'my people'—as far as he was concerned we were friends now, our alliance sealed by this daring cosmic confidence trick.

'All right then,' said Zaghloul, silencing the others with a raised hand. 'The people in your country—do they have a Holy Book, like we do?'

'Yes,' I said, pausing to think of an answer that would be both brief and undeniably true. 'Yes, they have several.'

'And do you have a Prophet, like we do?'

I answered with a quick nod, and having had enough of this conversation, I tried to turn it in a more agronomic direction, by asking a question about phosphates and rice-growing. But Zaghloul, as I was to discover later, had all the patient pertinacity that went with the weaver's craft and was not to be easily deflected once he had launched upon a subject.

'And who is your Prophet?' he said, ignoring my question. 'What is his name?'

I had no option now but to improvise; after a few moments of thought, I said: 'Al-Buddha.'

'Who?' cried Khamees. 'What was that you said?'

'Al-Buddha,' I repeated feebly, and Zaghloul looking at the others in stupefaction, said: 'Who can that be? All the world knows that Our Prophet, the Messenger of God, peace be on him, was the last and final Prophet. This is not a true prophet he is speaking of.'

Khamees leant over to tap me on my knee. 'All right then, ya doktór,' he said. 'Tell us something else then: is it true what they say? That you are a Magûsî, a Magian, and that in your country everybody worships cows? It is it true that the other day when you were walking through the fields you saw a man beating a cow and you were so upset you burst into tears and ran back to your room?'

'No, it's not true,' I said, but without much hope: I knew

from experience that there was nothing I could say that would effectively give the lie to this story. 'You're wrong. In my country people beat their cows all the time; I promise you.'

'So tell us then,' said someone else. 'In your country do you have military service, like we do in Egypt?'

'No,' I said, and in an effort to soften the shock of that revelation I began to explain that there were more than 700 million people in my country, and that if we'd had military service the army would have been larger than all of Egypt. But before I could finish Busaina interrupted me, throwing up her hands with a cry of despair.

'Everything's upside down in that country,' she said. 'Tell us, ya doktór: in your country do you at least have crops and fields and canals like we do?'

'Yes,' I said, 'we have crops and fields, but we don't always have canals. In some parts of my country they aren't needed because it rains all year around.'

'Ya salâm,' she cried, striking her forehead with the heel of her palm. 'Do you hear that, oh you people? Oh the Protector, oh, the Lord! It rains all the year around in his country.'

She had gone pale with amazement. 'So tell us then,' she demanded, 'do you have night and day like we do?'

'Shut up woman,' said Khamees. 'Of course they don't. It's day all the time over there, didn't you know? They arranged it like that so they wouldn't have to spend any money on lamps.'

After the laughter had died down, one of Khamees's brothers pointed to the baby who was now lying in the shade of a tree, swaddled in a sheet of cloth.

'That's Khamees's baby,' he said, with a grin. 'He was born last month.'

'That's wonderful,' I said: I had no idea then that he had

made me party to a savage joke at Khamees's expense. 'That's wonderful; Khamees must be very happy.'

Ignoring his brother, Khamees gave a cry of delight. 'The Indian knows,' he said. 'He understands that people are happy when they have children: he's not as upside down as we thought.'

He slapped me on the knee, grinning, and pushed forward his brother 'Eid, an exact miniaturized version of himself, no taller than his waist.

'Take this fellow with you when you go back, ya doktór, take him with you: all he does here is sit in the cornfields and play with himself.'

Stretching out a hand he squeezed the back of the boy's neck until he was squirming in discomfort. 'What would happen,' he said to me, 'if this boy 'Eid knocked on the door of your house in India and said: Is anyone there?'

'Someone would open the door,' I said, 'and my family would look after him.'

Khamees pulled a face: 'You mean they wouldn't set him on fire so that he wouldn't have to answer for his sins? What's the point of sending him then?'

Everyone else threw their heads back to laugh, but Busaina leaned across and patted my arm. 'You had better not go back,' she said, with an earnest frown. 'Stay here and become a Muslim and marry a girl from the village.'

Zaghloul was now rocking back and forth on his heels, frowning and shaking his head as though he had given up all hope of following the conversation.

'But tell me, ya doktór,' he burst out. 'Where is this country of yours? Can you go there in a day, like the people who go to Iraq and the Gulf?'

'You could,' I said, 'but my country is much further than Iraq, thousands of miles away.'

'Tell me something, ya doktór,' he said. 'If I got on to my donkey (if you'll pardon that word) and I rode and rode and rode for days, would I reach your country in the end?' He cocked his head to peer at me, as though the prospect of the journey had already filled him with alarm.

'No, ya Zaghloul,' I said, and then thinking of all the reasons why it would not be possible to travel from Egypt to India on a donkey, something caught fire in my imagination and I began to talk as I had never talked before, in Lataifa or Nashawy, of visas and quarantines, of the ribbon of war that stretched from Iraq to Afghanistan, of the heat of the Dasht-e-Kabir and the height of the Hindu Kush, of the foraging of snow leopards and the hairiness of yaks. No one listened to me more intently than Zaghloul, and for months afterwards, whenever he introduced me to anyone, he would tell them, with a dazzled, wondering lilt in his voice, of how far away my country was, of the deserts and wars and mountains that separated it from Egypt, and of the terrible fate that would befall one if one were to set out for it on a donkey.

To me there was something marvellous about the wonder that came into Zaghloul's voice when he talked of travel: for most of his neighbours travel held no surprises at all. The area around Nashawy had never been a rooted kind of place; at times it seemed to be possessed of all the busy restlessness of an airport's transit lounge. Indeed, a long history of travel was recorded in the very names of the area's 'families': they spoke of links with distant parts of the Arab world—cities in the Levant, the Sudan and the Maghreb. That legacy of transience had not ended with their ancestors either: in Zaghloul's own generation dozens of men had been 'outside', working in the shaikhdoms of the Gulf, or Libya, while many others had been to Saudi Arabia on the Hajj, or to the Yemen, as soldiers—some men had passports so thick they opened out like ink-blackened concertinas. But of course, Zaghloul and Khamees were eccentrics in most things, and in nothing so much as this, that for them the world outside was still replete with the wonders of the unknown. That was why our friendship was so quickly sealed.

9

FOR BEN YIJU the journey from Egypt towards Aden and India would have begun with a four-hundred-mile voyage down the Nile.

The trip could have taken as long as eighteen days since it meant sailing against the current; the same journey, in the other direction, could sometimes take as little as eight. The first leg of the eastward journey ended usually at one of several roadheads along the southern reaches of the Nile. In the twelfth century the largest and most frequently used of these was a place called Qus, now a modest district town a little north of Luxor. An Andalusian Arab, Ibn Jubaîr, who travelled this leg of the route some sixty years after Ben Yiju, spent a few weeks there while waiting for a camel caravan, for the next stage of his journey. He noted in his account that the town was admirably cosmopolitan, with many Yemeni, Ethiopian and Indian merchants passing through—'a station for the traveller, a gathering place for caravans, and a meeting-place for pilgrims.'

On Monday, 6 June 1183, he and his companions took their baggage to a palm-fringed spot on the outskirts of the town where other pilgrims and merchants had gathered to join a caravan. Their baggage was weighed and loaded on to camels, and the caravan set off after the evening prayers. Over the next seventeen days they progressed slowly through the desert, on a south-easterly tack, camping at night and travelling through the day. A well-marked trail of wells helped them on their way, and all along the route they passed caravans travelling in the opposite direction so that the barren and inhospitable wastes were 'animated and safe'. At one of the wells Ibn Jubair tried to count the caravans that passed by, but there were so many that he lost count. Much of their cargo consisted of goods from India; the loads of pepper, in particular, were so many 'as to seem to our fancies to equal the dust in quantity'.

It was a long, arduous journey, but there were ways of easing its rigours—for example, special litters called shaqâdîf, the best of which were made in the Yemen, large, roomy constructions, covered with leather inside, and provided with supports for a canopy. These litters were usually mounted in pairs, one balancing the other, so that two people could travel on each camel in relative comfort, shielded from the heat of the sun. Ibn Jubair remarked that 'whoso deems it lawful' could play chess with his companion while travelling, but as for himself he was on a pilgrimage, and being disinclined to spend his time on pursuits of questionable lawfulness, he spent the journey 'learning by heart the Book of Great and Glorious God.'

On 23 June, the caravan reached its destination, a Red Sea port on the coast of what is now northern Sudan. Fifty-three days had passed since Ibn Jubair had left Masr.

The port he had reached, 'Aidhâb, is one of the mysteries of the medieval trade route between Egypt and India. It was a tiny outpost, a handful of reed shacks and a few newly built plaster houses, marooned in a fierce and inhospitable stretch of desert. The area around it was inhabited by a tribe which regarded the merchants and pilgrims who passed through their territory with suspicion bordering on hostility. The sentiment was amply reciprocated by travellers like Ibn Jubair: 'Their men and women go naked abroad, wearing nothing but the rag which covers their genitals, and most not even this. In a word they are a breed of no regard and it is no sin to pour maledictions upon them.' Nothing grew in the harsh desert surroundings; everything had to be imported by ship, including water, which tasted so bitter when it arrived that Ibn Jubair found it 'less agreeable than thirst'. It was in every way a hateful, inhospitable place: 'A sojourn in it is the greatest snare on the road to [Mecca]... Men tell stories of its abominations, even saying that Solomon the son of David ...took it as a prison for the 'ifrît.'

Yet this little cluster of huts wedged between desert and sea was a busy, thriving port. Ibn Jubair himself, for all his dislike of the place, was among the many travellers who marvelled at the volume of Aidhab's traffic: 'It is one of the most frequented ports of the world, because of the ships of India and the Yemen that sail to it and from it, as well as the pilgrim ships that come and go.'

For about five hundred years Aidhab functioned as one of the most important halts on the route between the Indian Ocean and the Mediterranean. Then, suddenly, in the middle of the fifteenth century its life came to an end: it simply ceased to be, as though it had been erased from the map. The precise cause of its demise is uncertain, but it is possible that the port was destroyed on the orders of the then Sultan of Egypt. In any case, all that remains of it today are a few ruins and a great quantity of buried Chinese pottery.

A curious fragment, a piece of twelfth-century paper, links Abraham Ben Yiju to this doomed port. It contains an angry accusation against him, the only one of several such letters that has survived. It was not however sent to Ben Yiju himself. Cannily, the writer addressed it to the man who was in the best position to exercise an influence on Ben Yiju—his friend and mentor, the Nagid of merchants in Aden, Madmun ibn Bundar.

Madmun appears not to have taken the complaints very seriously at first, but the old man's sense of injury was deep enough to make him extraordinarily persistent. He wrote to Madmun again and again, and finally, in about 1135, when Ben Yiju had been in India at least three years, Madmun cut off a part of one of the letters and sent it on to Ben Yiju in Mangalore, along with a letter of his own.

Madmun's letter is a long one, one of the most important he ever wrote. It is only towards the end of it that he makes a cryptic reference to the note of complaint from Aidhab. 'The carrier of this letter,' he writes, 'will deliver to you a letter from Makhlûf al-Wutûm, which he sent from 'Aidhâb, and of which I already have more than 20…He is old and has become feeble-minded. He is reaching the end of his life and doesn't know how to go on.'

By an extraordinary coincidence it so happens that the letter has survived and is currently lodged, like Madmun's own, in the library of the University of Cambridge. It is written on a fragment of paper of good, if not the best, quality, more than a foot in length, and about four inches wide. The paper is considerably weathered and discoloured; it is torn at the top, and there is a small hole in it that looks as though it has been caused by a burn. But the writing, which extends all the way down both sides, is clear and can be read without difficulty: it is written in a distinctively Yemeni hand. The complaint is worded thus:

> Shaikh Abraham ibn Yijû bespoke the porterage of 5 bahârs from me. But every time I see him he crosses words with me, so that I have become frightened of him. Each time he says to me: Go, get out, perish…a hundred times…[My master Maḍmûn] deals with me according to his noble character and custom…I spoke previously to the ship-owner about this matter, and he told me I should turn to you…[I ask] of your Exalted Presence to act in this matter, until you reclaim the [money]…Stand by me in this, and strengthen your heart, O my lord and master…and extend your help to me…

Nothing else is known either about the writer of this letter or where the two men met. In any event the old man clearly felt that Ben Yiju owed him a large sum of money for transporting goods of the weight of five bahars. As it turned out he eventually even succeeded in persuading Madmun of his claims. Madmun's dismissive comments about the old man are probably nothing more than a gesture to spare Ben Yiju's feelings: he is hardly likely to have forwarded the letter all the way to Mangalore if he thought the old man's complaints to be entirely unfounded.

There is one last piece of evidence that bears upon the incident. It occurs in a later letter from Madmun to Ben Yiju. It consists of a brief entry on the debit side of Ben Yiju's account with Madmun. It says : 'For the affair of Shaikh Makhlûf, three hundred dînârs exactly.'

Evidently, Madmun was able to persuade Ben Yiju to pay off his insistent creditor.

10

AS IT TURNED out, Busaina had a hand in the events that led to my first meeting with the Imam—or a finger, more accurately, for it was largely by accident that she happened to embroil me in a conversation with the Imam's son at the village market.

It was no accident that the Imam's son, Yasir, happened to be there that morning, for by tradition his family had always had a special role to play in the Thursday souk. The market was held in the open threshing-ground beside the tomb of his ancestor, Sidi Abu-Kanaka, in exactly the same place as the saint's annual mowlid: in a way the mowlid and the market were a twinned pair, for although one was a weekly and the other an annual, one a largely secular and the other an avowedly spiritual event, by virtue of their location they both fell within the immediate sphere of the Sidi's blessings, and his benign presence stood surety for the exchanges of the market-place just as much as it guaranteed the sanctity of the mowlid. For that reason, it fell to his descendants, as the executors of his spiritual estate, so to speak, to collect a share of the proceeds of the market for the village. The organizing committee of the village mosque had authorized Yasir to sell tickets to every trader who came to the market, so that everyone who profited from the Thursday souk would also make a small contribution to the general betterment—towards the upkeep of the Saint's tomb, the maintenance of the village mosque and

179

perhaps even the relief effort in Afghanistan. At one time the Imam had collected the proceeds himself, but with advancing age and an increasing disinclination to spend his time on workaday business, he had delegated more and more of his responsibilities to his son, and now it was Yasir who made the rounds of the market on Thursday mornings.

Yasir was a pleasant, cheerful-looking person, and although our acquaintance had never proceeded beyond a few polite words, he always called out a friendly greeting when we passed each other in the lanes of the village. He was in his early forties or so, a tall, deep-chested man who, like his father, always wore a large, white turban—a species of headgear that was as distinctive of men who practised specialized trades as lace caps were of educated men, or woollen 'tageyyas' of the fellaheen. Like the old Imam, Yasir had learnt to cut hair and do everything else that went with the hereditary trade of his lineage, but while the Imam had never had much of a taste for barbering, Yasir, on the other hand, had taught himself to take a good deal of satisfaction in his craft. In his later years the Imam had driven away nearly all his customers; his increasing contempt for his profession eventually lent his razor so furious an edge that a time came when few men were willing to sit still with that agitated instrument hovering above their naked throats and bared armpits. But then, at just the right moment, Yasir had stepped in, and much as though he were the aberrantly conscientious son of a decaying industrial family, he had turned the business around and made it profitable.

In the years when the Imam had allowed his clients to drift away, several men had taken to barbering to make a little extra money. There were some half-dozen barbers in Nashawy now, who went from house to house, cutting their clients' hair and doling out injections for fifteen piastres a shot. But Yasir had started with an advantage over them in that he was the only man of his age in the village who could legitimately claim to have been born with the scissors in his fist. Upon coming to manhood he had made the best of his head-start by setting up a small barber-shop, the first in the entire area.

'Amm Taha had pointed it out to me once as we walked past. It was a simple enough affair; a little room with a couple of chairs, a wooden desk on which he kept his scissors and razors, a mirror hanging on one of the mud walls, and a few pictures for decoration, including a poster from a cinema theatre in Damanhour, of Raj Kapoor in *Sangam*.

There were those who had warned against the venture, 'Amm Taha said, for new-fangled ideas didn't generally go down well in Nashawy. There was the case of Shahata Bassiuni's café, for example: everyone had said it was a good idea to begin with, especially the young mowazzafeen who missed the coffee-houses they had got used to while studying in the city. So Shahata Bassiuni went ahead and set up a few iron tables and chairs, bought some narguilahs for those who wanted to smoke, and laid out a couple of chess and backgammon sets. As far as he was concerned, he was in business. But in the end all that came of it was that a few young layabouts took to spending their days hanging around his shop, ordering nothing and filching the chess pieces. A couple of times fights broke out too, and eventually, for the sake of his own peace of mind, Shahata Bassiuni had shut the place down.

'Amm Taha had laughed gleefully at the end of the story, giving me a suggestive little glance, to let it be known that if he had conspired with the dark powers that had taught Shahata Bassiuni his lesson, he would neither admit nor deny it. But even 'Amm Taha was willing to grant that Yasir had made a success of his barber-shop; so willing, in fact, that I was not surprised when Yasir began to whisper prayers to protect himself from envy upon encountering 'Amm Taha's eye as we walked past his shop.

Yasir's was now the only barber-shop in the area around Nashawy; the next one lay at a full truck-ride's distance, half-way to Damanhour. Over the past few years many men from nearby villages and hamlets had started coming to Yasir's shop—not just his father's old clients but even educated people like Ustaz Sabry, who could just as easily have gone to shops in the city. But despite his best efforts, Yasir had not yet succeeded in enticing college students like Nabeel or Isma'il into his shop; this was one instance in which they were not willing to follow Ustaz Sabry's lead. They would readily grant that Yasir was a perfectly good barber, more than adequate for the fellaheen and village folk but, as for themselves, they went on saving their coins in ones and twos, waiting for their monthly visit to the one shop in Damanhour which could be trusted to execute the styles they liked best.

Yasir's shop was in the front room of the small house that he and his family shared with his mother, the Imam's first wife. His mother had moved into the house when Yasir was just a boy, soon after the Imam took a second wife. The Imam was distraught with grief at the time, even though they'd only moved to the other side of the village square—Yasir was his only son and the thought of being separated from him was more than he could bear. In the end, taking pity on him, Yasir's mother allowed him to visit her house once a day, at the time of the midday meal. The arrangement stuck and ever afterwards Imam Ibrahim had walked over to their house once a day, after the noon-time prayers, to share his midday meal with his son and his grandchildren.

Yasir usually began work early in the morning, not long after the sunrise prayers and, depending on the flow of customers, he worked through till the midday prayers, when he went home to eat with his father. On Thursdays, however, his day was interrupted by the souk: he would close his shop for the morning, and with his ticket-book under his arm he would go out and plunge into the crowd of people swirling past his ancestor's tomb. Soon his white turban would be lost in the flood of colour that poured through the market-place on Thursdays: the flashing red of the butcher's tarpaulin, the cloth-sellers' bolts of parrot-green, scarlet and azure, the fish glittering on plastic sheets and the great black umbrella that hung slantwise over the man who repaired stoves. On other days the dun shades of the village's mud walls seemed thirsty for a touch of colour; Thursday mornings were the moments when that need was abundantly and extravagantly slaked.

The professional traders and vendors were usually the first to set up their stalls. They would begin to arrive early in the morning in their little donkey-carts, the fishmongers, the butchers, the fruit-sellers, the cloth-merchants, the watchmaker and a score of others of less determinate callings. The amateurs would follow a little later, women for the most part, swathed heavily in black, carrying wicker baskets loaded with tomatoes, carrots and cauliflowers, depending on the season. The moment they set foot in the market-place they would begin to call out greetings to their friends, to cousins from other villages and sisters who had married into faraway hamlets; they would spread out little sheets of plastic in the dust and pile them high with vegetables or fruit or whatever it was that they had gathered on their plots that morning and then, squatting behind their heaped wares, they would revive the innumerable interrupted relationships the market sustained from week to passing week.

The younger girls would do their best to be there too, slipping quietly out of their houses after their fathers and brothers had gone out to work on the fields; they would wander around the souk in groups, their hands around each others' waists, talking and laughing, and when they encountered a group of young men they would flounce past, holding their noses high, amidst explosions of bantering laughter.

On this particular Thursday the crowd had thinned by the time I went down to the market; it was already ten o'clock now, and most people had done their shopping earlier, while the vendors' wares were still fresh. Now, the time of day was beginning to show on the vegetables; the lettuce and watercress had wilted and the tomatoes were beginning to blister. Soon the prices would begin to tumble, when the women became impatient to set off for their homes in time to give their children their midday meals.

'What are you doing here?' a voice demanded as I stooped over a pile of knobbly carrots. 'Didn't I tell you to ask me if you wanted anything from the market?'

Looking up in surprise, I saw two diminutive women standing over me, their frowning faces framed by heavy black robes. The smaller of the two was Ustaz Sabry's mother, and her eyes darted from my face to the carrots in my hand as she leant over to look at me.

'What will you do with those carrots?' she shot at me, glaring, as though she had chanced upon a dark secret.

'I'll eat them,' I answered.

'How?'

'I may eat them raw,' I said, 'or I may cook them if I feel like it.'

'Cook them?' she said, frowning. 'What will you cook them on? Have you got a stove?'

'Yes.'

'What sort of stove do you have?'

'A kerosene stove.'

'A kerosene stove! And what do you cook on your kerosene stove?'

'Many things—rice for example; I cook rice.'

'How do you cook your rice?' she said, smiling sweetly. 'Do you cook it with milk?'

'Yes,' I declared recklessly, anxious to establish my self-sufficiency. 'Sometimes I cook it with milk.'

'But how?' she said. 'Don't you know you have to have an oven to cook rice with milk?'

She shook her head sadly as I floundered for an answer. 'What will you do with your stove when you go?' she demanded.

'Why don't you give it to me?' said the other woman.

'No he won't,' said Ustaz Sabry's mother, casting her a significant look. 'It's no use asking: old Taha must have his eyes on it already.'

She began to stroke my arm with a maternal weariness. 'Tell me my son,' she said, 'when are you going back home? Isn't your holiday over yet?'

Summoning my dignity as best I could, I told her I was not on holiday; what I was doing was work, serious work (secretly I had begun to have doubts on that score, but I wasn't going to admit them to her). I still had a lot of work to do, I insisted,

185

and it would be several more months before I was finished.

'Your poor mother,' she said. 'She must miss you so much.'

Still stroking my arm she flashed her friend a smile.

'He is very fond of cows,' she told her. 'He often goes down to the fields to take pictures of cows.'

Her friend nearly dropped her cauliflowers as she spun around to look at me, her mouth falling open in amazement.

'Yes,' said Ustaz Sabry's mother, nodding knowledgeably. 'He goes down to the fields whenever he hears the cows are out. He goes with his camera and he takes pictures of cows—and sheep and goats and camels.'

'And people too,' I added reproachfully.

She pursed her lips as though that were a subject on which she would prefer to reserve judgement. Her eyes in the meanwhile had fastened upon a distant cabbage, but before shuffling off to bargain for it she gave my arm a final parting pat. 'You must come to us whenever you want anything,' she said. 'Sabry so much likes to talk to you—why, just the other day he said to me, the people of Egypt and India have been like brothers for centuries. You must consider yourself one of our family.'

I turned back to the carrots as she went off to hunt down her cabbage, but no sooner had I begun to pick through the pile than I was interrupted once again.

'Over here, ya doktór,' a voice called out to me. 'Come over here.' It was Busaina, sitting cross-legged behind her own plastic sheet, waving a bunch of green coriander.

'Here, ya doktór,' she said. 'Come and buy some things from over here so I can say khalas and make my way home.'

My very first glance at the collection of vegetables in front of her told me that they were the most miserable in the market: a few fraying heads of lettuce, some ragged bunches of watercress and a heap of soggy onions mixed with a few other scraps. Unlike the other piles in the row, hers didn't consist of remnants from the morning's sales: it was so large that it was clear that she had sold hardly anything at all.

It had happened to her before, 'Amm Taha told me later; her vegetables were often untouched at the end of the morning. It wasn't her salesmanship that was to blame—she was, if anything, a real professional, the only woman in the market who actually made a living by selling vegetables. Her problem was that her vegetables did not come directly from the fields— she gathered them in bits and pieces, going from house to house and buying leftovers. It wasn't often that she could bring vegetables from her own family's land, for there were so many people in their household that they rarely had anything to sell. When they did, it was her brothers' wives who usually brought them to the market; that was their privilege as the wives of the house, and Busaina, as a sister, had to fend for herself.

Her family had welcomed her back after she left her husband, and according to the custom of the village they had given her all the support they could, and would go on doing so, even if her husband did not meet his obligation to send money for the children. But she for her part had begun to look for work the moment she arrived, for she wasn't willing to let her children be raised as dependants in her brothers' household. She had known, when she left her husband, that she was entering upon virtual widowhood, for although she was still in her twenties it was almost a certainty that, as the mother of two young children, she would not be able to marry again. Having renounced wifely domesticity, she had become doubly ambitious for her sons and had begun to work long hours carrying her basket around all the markets in the nearby villages.

'What am I going to do, ya doktór?' she said, flicking the flies off her vegetables with a loud, full-throated laugh. 'I'll have to throw these things into the canal—maybe the catfish will want to eat them.'

Her hilarity increased when I picked out a bunch of watercress and held out a twenty-five piastre note. 'I'll save some of that for my son's wedding,' she said, and her shoulders shook as she handed me my change.

A few minutes later, when I was bargaining over a bunch of grapes with a travelling fruit-vendor from Damanhour, I was taken by surprise to hear her voice, shouting angrily over my shoulder.

'Say that again, boss,' she challenged the fruit vendor. 'I want to hear you say that again. Fifty piastres for that rotten bunch— is that what you want to charge him?'

The vendor stood his ground, but a sheepish look came over him as he began to explain that it wasn't his fault, things were getting more and more expensive day by day, and he had to come all the way from Damanhour in his donkey-cart. 'And besides,' he ended lamely, his voice rising to a high-pitched whine, 'they're good grapes, you just try them and see.'

'"Good grapes",' mimicked Busaina. 'So if they're so good why don't you keep them yourself?'

'Wallahi,' swore the vendor, pointing a finger heavenwards. 'I'm not asking too much—that's exactly what it costs.'

'I go to the market every day,' said Busaina. 'Don't try to fool me. I know, you're having fun at his expense.'

'But he's from the city,' the vendor protested. 'Why shouldn't he pay city prices—since he'll only take them back with him?'

'He lives here now,' said Busaina, 'he's not in the city any more.' She snatched the grapes out of my hand and thrust them back on to his cart. 'Thirty piastres, not a girsh more.'

'Never,' said the vendor, with an outraged yell. 'Never, never—I'd rather divorce my wife!'

'Why don't you do it?' shouted Busaina. 'You'll see: she'll clap her hands and cry "Praise God".'

That was when Yasir appeared, just as an audience was beginning to collect around us. Through his adjudication Busaina was vindicated and order restored, and after she had gone triumphantly back to her pile of vegetables, Yasir and I had a long conversation which ended with his offering to take me to meet his father, Imam Ibrahim, at any time of my choosing.

11

TAKING YASIR AT his word I stopped at his shop one morning, several days later. He was busy with a client, but he immediately laid down his razor and offered to lead me to his father's house, on the far side of the village square.

He had let Imam Ibrahim know that I wanted to talk to him, he said, so my visit would not be unexpected. He would have liked to stay himself, to listen to me talking to his father, but of course he couldn't leave his shop for long.

'But come and eat with us this afternoon,' he said with a smile, leading me across the square. 'Come after the midday prayers. My father will be there too, insha'allah, so we can sit together and discuss all kinds of matters.'

The Imam's house was directly opposite the mosque, squeezed in amongst a maze of low huts, each crowned with a billowing head of straw. Yasir rapped hard on his heavy, wooden door and after making sure that someone was stirring inside, he hurried back towards his shop, with another quick reminder about eating at his house at midday.

I listened for a while, and then knocked again, gingerly. A moment later the door swung open, and the Imam was standing directly in front of me. He was dressed in a mud-stained blue jallabeyya, with his turban knotted haphazardly around his head; a tall man, and somehow bigger than he had seemed at a distance, deep-chested and burly, with a broad pair of shoulders and long, busy fingers that kept fidgeting with his buttonholes and sleeves. There was something unkempt about his appearance, a look of mild disarray, yet his short white beard was neatly trimmed, and his brown eyes were bright with a sharp and impatient intelligence. Age had been harsh on him, but there was still an unmistakable energy about the way he carried himself; it was easy to see that he had long been accustomed to swaying audiences through the sheer force of his presence.

'Welcome,' he said, inclining his head. His tone was stiffly formal and there was no trace of a smile on his face.

Standing aside, he waved me through and once I was in he pulled the door shut behind him. I found myself in a small, dark room with mud walls that sloped and bulged like sodden riverbanks. The room was very bare; it held a bed, a couple of mats, and a few books and utensils, all uniformly covered with a thin patina of grime.

'Welcome,' said the Imam, holding his right hand stiffly and formally over his heart.

'Welcome to you,' I said in response, and then we began on the usual litany of greetings.

'How are you?'

'How are you?'

'You have brought blessings.'

'May God bless you.'

'Welcome.'

'Welcome to you.'

'You have brought light.'

'The light is yours.'

'How are you?'

'How are you?'

He prolonged the ritual well past its usual duration, and as soon as we had exhausted the list of salutations, he pulled out a kerosene stove and began to pump it in preparation for brewing tea. At length, after lighting the stove and measuring the tea and water, when conversation could no longer be forestalled, he turned to me stiffly and said: 'So you're the doktór al-Hindi?'

Yes, I said, and then I explained that I had come to talk to him about his methods of healing, and, if he wished, about his ancestors and the history of his family. He was taken by surprise; he stirred the kettle silently for a while and then began again on the ritual of greetings and responses, as though to pre-empt any further discussion.

'Welcome.'

'Welcome to you.'

'You have brought light.'

'The light is yours.'

We went slowly through the list of greetings and at the end of it, determined not to be shaken off, I repeated again that I was greatly interested in learning about folk remedies and herbal medicines, and I had heard that no one knew more about the subject than he. I had thought that he might perhaps be flattered, but in fact his response was one of utter dismay.

'Who told you those things?' he demanded to know, as though I had relayed an unfounded and slanderous accusation. 'Who was it? Tell me.'

'Why, everyone,' I stammered. 'So many people say that you know a great deal about remedies; that is why I came to you to learn about herbs and medicine.'

'Why do you want to hear about my herbs?' he retorted. 'Why don't you go back to your country and find out about your own?'

'I will,' I said. 'Soon. But right now...'

'No, no,' he said impatiently. 'Forget about all that; I'm trying to forget about it myself.'

Reaching over, he poured out two glasses of tea and, after handing me one, he emptied the other in a couple of mouthfuls. Then, falling to his knees, he reached under his bed and brought out a glistening new biscuit tin.

'Here,' he said, thrusting the open box in front of me. 'Look!'

Half a dozen phials and a hypodermic syringe lay inside the box, nestling in a bed of soiled cotton wool. His eyes shone as he gazed at them: this is what he had been learning over the last few years, he said, the art of mixing and giving injections —he had long since forgotten about herbs and poultices. There was a huge market for injections in the village; everyone wanted one, for colds and fevers and dysentery and so many other things. There was a good living in it; it was where the future lay.

He seemed to change as he talked; he did not seem like an old man any more; he was rejuvenated, renewed by the sight of his needle and syringe, lying in their box like talismans of times yet to come.

I knew then that he would never talk to me about the remedies he had learned from his father; not merely because he was suspicious of me and my motives, but also because those medicines were even more discredited in his own eyes than they were in everyone else's; the mere mention of them was as distasteful to him as talk of home to an exile. The irony was that he, who was no more than a walking fossil, a relic of the past, in the eyes of Nabeel and his generation, was actually on fire with a vision of the future.

'Let me show you,' he said, and picking up his syringe, he reached for my arm, eager to demonstrate his skills. I snatched my sleeve away, edging backwards, protesting that I wasn't ill and didn't need an injection, perhaps later, one day when I wasn't feeling well. He squinted at me, narrowing his eyes, and then, packing his syringe away, he rose to his feet.

'I have to go to the mosque right now,' he said. 'It's time for the midday prayers. Perhaps we can talk about this some other day, but right now I'm busy and I have to go.' He ushered me quickly out of the house, and then, at the steps of the mosque, he gave my hand a perfunctory shake and ran up the stairs, vanishing before I could tell him that he was not quite rid of me yet, and that we would be eating together at his son's house a short while later.

When we met again at Yasir's house, an hour or so later, he seemed more affable and not in the least bit put out to see me. We sat down around a tray in the guest-room, with Yasir's children playing around us. Afterwards, mellowed by the food, holding one child on his knee and another on his shoulder, he began to talk about his own, distant boyhood. He told stories I had often heard before from the older people in the village: of how, in the old days, everybody in the village, children included, would walk every morning to an estate that belonged to a rich Pasha from Alexandria, and of how they had worked through till sunset for a couple of piastres, sweating in the cotton fields under the gaze of armed overseers whose whips would come crashing down on their shoulders at the slightest sign of fatigue or slackness. Those were terrible times, he said, before Jamal 'Abd al-Nâṣir and the Revolution of 1952, when the Pashas, the King and their 'kindly uncles', the British army, had had their way in all things and the fellaheen had been forced to labour at their orders, like flies, working without proper recompense. Why, even in Nashawy, for a full score of years before the Revolution, the village had been ruled like a personal fiefdom by the old 'omda, a Badawy headman (the very man whose house I was living in) who had considered everything and everyone in the village his personal property. No one had been safe from his anger, and no one had dared stand up to him.

Yasir's children began to laugh; reared as they were, in free schools, with medical care abundantly and cheaply available, stories of those times had the mythical quality of a dark fairytale. But Yasir, who was a boy at the time of the revolution and was just old enough to remember those days, had turned sombre, as people of his age always did when they heard their elders talk of the past.

'Alḥamdu'lillah,' said Yasir, 'God be praised, all that was long ago, and now Egypt is a free country and we are all at liberty to do as we please.'

If I had not lived in Nashawy I might well have wondered whether he was being entirely serious in using those sonorous, oddly parliamentary phrases. But now, having been there, I understood very well that he meant exactly what he said, although it was not the whole range of classical liberal freedoms that he had in mind. He was really referring to the deliverance from forced labour that the Revolution of 1952 had ensured: to the fellaheen their most cherished liberty was that which had been most cruelly abused by the regimes of the past—their right to dispose freely of their worktime. It was a simple enough dispensation, but one for which every fellah of an age to remember the past was deeply and unreservedly grateful.

In a while Yasir's mother, the Imam's first wife, brought in a tray of tea, and after the glasses had been handed around, she sat with us and began to talk about her daughter and how, after her marriage, she had settled in a village that was so far away that now she had nobody for company except Yasir's wife and children.

I was still thinking about the stories I had just heard, listening to her with only half an ear, and when there was a lull in the conversation, I turned to Yasir absent-mindedly, and said: 'So you have only one sister then? No brothers at all?'

There was a sudden hush; Yasir's mother gasped, and Yasir himself cast a stricken glance at his father, sitting across the room. After what seemed an age of silence, he cleared his throat and, holding his right hand over his heart, he said: 'It is all the same, my father has given me one sister and there is no reproach if he has not been blessed with any sons other than I.'

The tone of his voice told me that I had trespassed unwarily on some deeply personal grief, something that had perhaps haunted their family for years. Knowing that I had committed a solecism for which I could never hope to make amends, I kept my silence and willed myself to stay sitting, exactly as I was.

'And my father has married again,' said Yasir, in an unnaturally loud voice. 'And since he is still in the full fitness of age, he may beget brothers for me yet…'

Imam Ibrahim did not allow him to finish. He threw a single frowning glance in my direction and stalked out of the room.

12

USING HIS POWERS, 'Amm Taha foretold the events of Nabeel's brother's wedding ceremony the morning before it was held. There would be lots of young people around their house, he said: all the young, unmarried boys and girls of the village, singing and dancing without a care in the world. But the supper would be a small affair, attended mainly by relatives and guests from other villages. Old Idris, Nabeel's father, had invited a lot of people from Nashawy too, for their family was overjoyed about the marriage and wanted to celebrate it as best they could. But many of the people he had invited wouldn't go, out of consideration for the old man, to cut down his expenses— everyone knew their family couldn't really afford a big wedding. Their younger friends and relatives would drop by during the day and then again in the evening, mainly to dance and sing. They would be outside in the lanes; they wouldn't go into the house with the guests—the supper was only for elders and responsible, grown-up men.

'They'll start arriving in the morning, insha'allah,' said 'Amm Taha, 'and by the time you get there they'll all be sitting in the guest-room. They'll want to talk to you, for none of them will ever have met an Indian before.'

My heart sank when I realized that for me the evening would mean a prolonged incarceration in a small, crowded room. 'I would rather be outside,' I said, 'watching the singing and dancing.'

'Amm Taha laughed with a hint of malign pleasure, as though he had already glimpsed a wealth of discomfiture lying in wait for me in his divinations of the evening ahead. 'They won't let you stay outside,' he said. 'You're a kind of effendi, so they'll make you go in and sit with the elders and all the other guests.'

I tried to prove him wrong when I went to Nabeel's house that evening, and for a short while, at the beginning, I actually thought I'd succeeded.

By the time I made my way there, a large crowd had gathered in the lane outside and I merged gratefully into its fringes. There were some forty or fifty boys and girls there, packed in a tight semicircle in front of the bride and groom. The newly-married couple were sitting on raised chairs, enthroned with their backs against the house, while their friends and relatives danced in front of them. The groom, 'Ali, was dressed in a new jallabeyya of brown wool, a dark, sturdily built young man, with a generous, open smile and a cleft in his chin. His bride and cousin, Fawzia, was wearing a white gown, with a frill of lace and a little gauzy veil. Her face had been carefully and evenly painted, so that her lips, cheeks, and ears were all exactly the same shade of iridescent pink. The flatness of the paint had created a curious effect, turning her face into a pallid, spectral mask: I was astonished to discover later that she was in fact a cheerful, good-looking woman, with a warm smile and a welcoming manner.

A boy was kneeling beside her chair, pounding out a

deafening, fast-paced rhythm upon a tin wash-basin that was propped against his leg. Someone was dancing in front of him, but the crowd was so thick around them that from where I stood I could see little more than the bobbing of the dancer's head. Bracing myself against a wall, I rose on tiptoe and saw that the dancer was a boy, one of Nabeel's cousins; he was dancing bawdily, jerking his hips in front of the girls, while some of his friends reached out to slap him on his buttocks, doubling over with laughter at his coquettish twitching.

All around me voices were chanting the words of a refrain that invoked the voluptuous fruitfulness of pomegranates—'Ya rummân, ya rummân'—and with every word, dozens of hands came crashing together, clapping in unison, in perfect time with the beat. The spectators were jostling for a better view now, the boys balancing on each others' shoulders, the girls climbing upon the window-sills. The dance was approaching its climax when Nabeel appeared at my side; followed by his father. After a hurried exchanged of greetings, they put their arms through mine and led me firmly back towards their house.

The moment I stepped into their smoky, crowded guest-room, I knew that I was in for a long interrogation: I had a premonition of its coming in the strained boredom on the faces of the men who were assembled there, in the restlessness of their fidgeting fingers and their tapping toes, as they sat in silence in that hot, sweaty room, while the lanes around them resounded with the clamour of celebration. They turned to face me as I walked in, all of them together, some fifteen or twenty men, grateful for the distraction, for the temporary rupture with the uncomfortably intimate world evoked by the songs outside, the half-forgotten longings and reawakened desires, the memories of fingers locking in secret and hands brushing against hips in the surging crowd—all the village's young and unmarried, boys and girls together, thronging around the dancers, clapping and chanting, intoxicated with the heightened eroticism of the wedding night, that feverish air whose mysteries I had just begun to sense when Nabeel and his father spotted me in the crowd and led me away to face this contingent of fidgeting, middle-aged men sitting in their guest-room.

I looked around quickly, searching for a familiar face, but to my dismay I discovered that they were all outsiders, from other villages, and that I knew no one there, no one at all, since Nabeel and his father had gone back to their post outside to receive their guests. There were a few moments of silent scrutiny and then the man beside me cleared his throat and asked whether I was the doctor who had recently been posted to the government clinic.

A look of extreme suspicion came into his eyes when I explained my situation, and as soon as I had finished he began to fire off a series of questions—about how I had learnt Arabic, and who had brought me to Nashawy, and whether I had permission from the Government of Egypt. No sooner had I given him the answers than he demanded to see my identity card, and when I explained that I did not have a card, but I did indeed have an official letter from the Ministry of the Interior which I would gladly show him if he would accompany me to my room, his face took on an expression of portentous seriousness and he began to mutter direly about spies and impostors and a possible report to the Mukhabbarât, the intelligence wing of the police.

He was quickly elbowed away however, for there were many others around him who were impatient now, brimming with questions of their own. Within moments a dozen or so people had crowded around me, and I was busy affirming that yes, in my country there were indeed crops like rice and wheat, and yes, in India too, there were peasants like the fellaheen of Egypt, who lived in adobe villages and turned the earth with cattle-drawn ploughs. The questions came ever faster, even as I was speaking: 'Are most of your houses still built of mud-brick as they are here?' and 'Do your people cook on gas stoves or do they still burn straw and wood as we do?'

I grew increasingly puzzled as I tried to deal with this barrage of inquiries, first, by the part the word 'still' played in their questions, and secondly by the masks of incredulity that seemed to fall on their faces as I affirmed, over and over again, that yes, in India too people used cattle-drawn ploughs and not tractors; water-wheels and not pumps; donkey-carts, not trucks, and yes, in India too there were many, many people who were very poor, indeed there were millions whose poverty they would scarcely have been able to imagine. But to my utter bewilderment, the more I insisted, the more sceptical they seemed to become, until at last I realized, with an overwhelming sense of shock, that the simple truth was that they did not believe what I was saying.

I later came to understand that their disbelief had little or nothing to do with what I had said; rather, they had constructed a certain ladder of 'Development' in their minds, and because all their images of material life were of those who stood in the rungs above, the circumstances of those below had become more or less unimaginable. I had an inkling then of the real and desperate seriousness of their engagement with modernism, because I realized that the fellaheen saw the material circumstances of their lives in exactly the same way that a university economist would: as a situation that was shamefully anachronistic, a warp upon time; I understood that their relationships with the objects of their everyday lives was never innocent of the knowledge that there were other places, other countries which did not have mud-walled houses and cattle-drawn ploughs, so that those objects, those houses and ploughs, were insubstantial things, ghosts displaced in time, waiting to be exorcized and laid to rest. It was thus that I had my first suspicion of what it might mean to belong to an 'historical civilization', and it left me bewildered because, for my own part, it was precisely the absoluteness of time and the discreteness of epochs that I always had trouble in imagining.

The supper was a quick affair; about ten of us were taken to another room, at the back, where we helped ourselves to lamb, rice and sweetmeats standing around a table, and as soon as we had eaten, we were led out again and another lot of guests was brought in. I decided to take advantage of the bustle, and while Nabeel and his father were busy leading their guests back and forth, I slipped out of the guest-room and back into the lane.

It was long past sunset now, and the faces around the bridal couple were glowing under a dome of dust that had turned golden in the light of a single kerosene lamp. The drum-beat on the wash-basin was a measured, gentle one and when I pushed my way into the centre of the crowd I saw that the dancer was a young girl, dressed in a simple, printed cotton dress, with a long scarf tied around her waist. Both her hands were on her hips, and she was dancing with her eyes fixed on the ground in front of her, moving her hips with a slow, languid grace, backwards and forwards while the rest of her body stayed still, almost immobile, except for the quick, circular motion of her feet. Then gradually, almost imperceptibly, the tempo of the beat quickened, and somebody called out the first line of a chant, *khadnâha min wasaṭ al-dâr*, 'we took her from her father's house,' and the crowd shouted back, *wa abûha gâ'id za'alân*, 'while her father sat there bereft.' Then the single voice again, *khadnâha bi al-saif al-mâḍî*, 'we took her with a sharpened sword,' followed by the massed refrain, *wa abûha makânsh râḍî*, 'because her father wouldn't consent.'

The crowd pressed closer with the quickening of the beat, and as the voices and the clapping grew louder, the girl, in response, raised an arm and flexed it above her head in a graceful arc. Her body was turning now, rotating slowly in the same place, her hips moving faster while the crowd around her clapped and stamped, roaring their approval at the tops of their voices. Gradually, the beat grew quicker, blurring into a tattoo of drumbeats, and in response her torso froze into stillness, while her hips and her waist moved ever faster, in exact counterpoint, in a pattern of movement that became a perfect abstraction of eroticism, a figurative geometry of lovemaking, pounding back and forth at a dizzying speed until at last the final beat rang out and she escaped into the crowd, laughing.

'Where have you been all this while?' a voice cried out behind me. 'We have been looking everywhere for you—there's so much still to ask.'

Turning around I came face to face with the man who had demanded to see my identity card. Nabeel was following close behind, and between the two of them they led me back, remonstrating gently with me for having left the guest-room without warning.

There was a thick fog of smoke in the room when we went back in, for the wedding guests had lit cigarettes and shushas now and settled back on the divans to rest after the supper. Nabeel's father handed me a shusha of my own, and while I was trying to coax my coal into life, my interlocutors gathered around me again, and the questions began to flow once more.

'Tell us then,' said someone, 'in your country, amongst your people, what do you do with your dead?'

'They are burned,' I said, puffing stoically on my shusha as they recoiled in shock.

'And the ashes?' another voice asked. 'Do you at least save the ashes so that you can remember them by something?'

'No,' I said. 'No: even the ashes are scattered in the rivers.'

There was a long silence for it took a while before they could overcome their revulsion far enough to speak. 'So are they all unbelievers in your country?' someone asked at last. 'Is there no Law or Morality: can everyone do as they please—take a woman off the streets or sleep with another man's wife?'

'No,' I began, but before I could complete my answer I was cut short.

'So what about circumcision?' a voice demanded, and was followed immediately by another, even louder one, which wanted to know whether women in my country were 'purified' as they were in Egypt.

The word 'to purify' makes a verbal equation between male circumcision and clitoridectomy, being the same in both cases, but the latter is an infinitely more dangerous operation, since it requires the complete excision of the clitoris. Clitoridectomy is, in fact, hideously painful and was declared illegal after the Revolution, although it still continues to be widely practised, by Christian and Muslim fellaheen alike.

'No,' I said, 'women are not "purified" in my country.' But my questioner, convinced that I had not understood what he had asked, repeated his words again, slowly.

The faces around me grew blank with astonishment as I said 'no' once again. 'So you mean you let the clitoris just grow and grow?' a man asked, hoarse-voiced.

I began to correct him, but he was absorbed in his own amazement, and in the meanwhile someone else interrupted, with a sudden shout: 'And boys?' he cried, 'what about boys, are they not purified either?'

'And you, ya doktór?'

'What about you…?'

I looked at the eyes around me, alternately curious and horrified, and I knew that I would not be able to answer. My limbs seemed to have passed beyond my volition as I rose from the divan, knocking over my shusha. I pushed my way out, and before anyone could react, I was past the crowd, walking quickly back to my room.

I was almost there, when I heard footsteps close behind me. It was Nabeel, looking puzzled and a little out of breath.

'What happened?' he said. 'Why did you leave so suddenly?'

I kept walking for I could think of no answer.

'They were only asking questions,' he said, 'just like you do; they didn't mean any harm. Why do you let this talk of cows and burning and circumcision worry you so much? These are just customs; it's natural that people should be curious. These are not things to be upset about.'

13

I SOMETIMES WISHED I had told Nabeel a story.

When I was a child we lived in a place that was destined to fall out of the world's atlas like a page ripped in the press: it was East Pakistan, which, after its creation in 1947, survived only a bare twenty-five years before becoming a new nation, Bangladesh. No one regretted its passing; if it still possesses a life in my memory it is largely by accident, because my father happened to be seconded to the Indian diplomatic mission in Dhaka when I was about six years old.

There was an element of irony in our living in Dhaka as 'foreigners', for Dhaka was in fact our ancestral city: both my parents were from families which belonged to the middle-class Hindu community that had once flourished there. But long before the Muslim-majority state of Pakistan was created my ancestors had moved westwards, and thanks to their wanderlust we were Indians now, and Dhaka was foreign territory to us although we still spoke its dialect and still had several relatives living in the old Hindu neighbourhoods in the heart of the city.

The house we had moved into was in a new residential suburb on the outskirts of the city. The area had only recently been developed and when we moved there it still looked like a version of a planner's blueprint, with sketchy lots and lightly pencilled roads. Our house was spanking new; it was one of the first to be built in the area. It had a large garden, and high walls ran all the way around it, separating the compound from an expanse of excavated construction sites. There was only one other house nearby; the others were all at the end of the road, telescopically small, visible only with shaded eyes and a squint. To me they seemed remote enough for our house to be a desert island, with walls instead of cliffs.

At times, unaccountably, the house would fill up with strangers. The garden, usually empty except for dragonflies and grasshoppers, would be festooned with saris drying in the breeze, and there would be large groups of men, women and children sitting on the grass, with little bundles of clothes and pots and pans spread out beside them. To me, a child of seven or eight, there always seemed to be an air of something akin to light-heartedness about those people, something like relief perhaps; they would wave to me when I went down to the garden and sometimes the women would reach into their bundles and find me sweets. In the evenings, large fires would be lit in the driveway and my mother and her friends would stand behind huge cooking-pots, ladles in hand, the ends of their saris tucked in purposefully at the waist, serving out large helpings of food. We would all eat together, sitting around the garden as though it were a picnic, and afterwards we, the children, would play football and hide-and-seek. Then after a day or two everyone would be gone, the garden would be reclaimed by dragonflies and grasshoppers and peace would descend once more upon my island.

I was never surprised or put out by these visitations. To me they seemed like festive occasions, especially since we ate out of green banana leaves, just as we did at weddings and other celebrations. No one ever explained to me what those groups of people were doing in our house and I was too young to work out for myself that they were refugees, fleeing from mobs, and that they had taken shelter in our garden because ours was the only 'Hindu' house nearby that happened to have high walls.

On one particular day (a day in January 1964, I was to discover many years later) more people than ever before appeared in the garden, suddenly and without warning. They began to pour in early in the morning, in small knots, carrying bundles and other odds and ends, and as the day wore on the heavy steel gates of the house were opened time and time again to let more people in. By evening the garden was packed with people, some squatting in silent groups and others leaning against the walls, as though in wait.

Just after sunset, our cook came looking for me in the garden, and led me away, past the families that were huddled on the staircase and in the corridors, to my parents' bedroom, upstairs. By the time we got to the room, the shutters of all the windows had been closed, and my father was pacing the floor, waiting for me. He made me sit down, and then, speaking in a voice that could not be argued with, he told me to stay where I was. I was not to leave the bedroom on any account, he said, until he came back to fetch me. To make sure, he left our cook sitting by the door, with strict instructions not to leave his post.

As a rule I would have been perfectly happy to stay there with our cook, for he was a wonderful story-teller and often kept me entranced for hours on end, spinning out fables in the dialect of his region—long, epic stories about ghosts and ghouls and faraway lands where people ate children. He was from one of the maritime districts of East Pakistan and he had come to work with us because he had lost most of his family in the riots that followed Partition and now wanted to emigrate to India. He had learnt to cook on the river-steamers of his region, which were famous throughout Bengal for the quality of their cooking. After his coming the food in our house had become legendary amongst our family's friends. As for me, I regarded him with an equal mixture of fear and fascination, for although he was a small wiry man, he seemed bigger than he was because he had large, curling moustaches which made him somehow mysterious and menacing. When I tried to imagine the ghouls and spirits of his stories, they usually looked very much like him.

But today he had no stories to tell; he could hardly keep still and every so often he would go to the windows and look outside, prising the shutters open. Soon, his curiosity got the better of him and, after telling me to stay where I was, he slipped out of the room, forgetting to shut the door behind him. I waited a few minutes, and when he didn't come back, I ran out of the bedroom to a balcony which looked out over the garden and the lane.

My memories of what I saw are very vivid, but at the same time oddly out of synch, like a sloppily edited film. A large crowd is thronging around our house, a mob of hundreds of men, their faces shining red in the light of the burning torches in their hands, rags tied on sticks, whose flames seem to be swirling against our walls in waves of fire. As I watch, the flames begin to dance around the house, and while they circle the walls the people gathered inside mill around the garden, cower in huddles and cover their faces. I can see the enraged mob and the dancing flames with a vivid, burning clarity, yet all of it happens in utter silence; my memory, in an act of benign protection, has excised every single sound.

I do not know how long I stood there, but suddenly our cook rushed in and dragged me away, back to my parents' bedroom. He was shaken now, for he had seen the mob too, and he began to walk back and forth across the room, covering his face and tugging at his moustache.

In frustration at my imprisonment in that room, I began to disarrange the bedclothes. I pulled off the covers and began to tug at the sheets, when suddenly my father's pillow fell over, revealing a dark, metallic object. It was small, no larger than a toy pistol but much heavier, and I had to use both my hands to lift it. I pointed it at the wall, as I would my own water-pistol, and curling a finger around the trigger I squeezed as hard as I could. But nothing happened, there was no sound and the trigger wouldn't move. I tried once more, and again nothing happened. I turned it over in my hands, wondering what made it work, but then the door flew open and my father came into the room. He crossed the floor with a couple of strides, and snatched the revolver out of my hands. Without another word, he slipped it into his pocket and went racing out of the room.

It was then that I realized he was afraid we might be killed that night, and that he had sent me to the bedroom so I would be the last to be found if the gates gave way and the mob succeeded in breaking in.

But nothing did happen. The police arrived at just the right moment, alerted by some of my parents' Muslim friends, and drove the mob away. Next morning, when I looked out over the balcony, the garden was strewn with bricks and rubble, but the refugees who had gathered there were sitting peacefully in the sun, calm, though thoroughly subdued.

Our cook, on the other hand, was in a mood of great elation that morning, and when we went downstairs he joked cheerfully with the people in the garden, laughing, and asking how they happened to be there. Later, we squatted in a corner and he whispered in my ear, pointing at the knots of people around us, and told me their stories. I was to recognize those stories years later, when reading through a collection of old newspapers, I discovered that on the very night when I'd seen those flames dancing around the walls of our house, there had been a riot in Calcutta too, similar in every respect except that there it was Muslims who had been attacked by Hindus. But equally, in both cities—and this must be said, it must always be said, for it is the incantation that redeems our sanity—in both Dhaka and Calcutta, there were exactly mirrored stories of Hindus and Muslims coming to each others' rescue, so that many more people were saved than killed.

The stories of those riots are always the same: tales that grow out of an explosive barrier of symbols—of cities going up in flames because of a cow found dead in a temple or a pig in a mosque; of people killed for wearing a lungi or a dhoti, depending on where they find themselves; of women disembowelled for wearing veils or vermilion, of men dismembered for the state of their foreskins.

But I was never able to explain very much of this to Nabeel or anyone else in Nashawy. The fact was that despite the occasional storms and turbulence their country had seen, despite even the wars that some of them had fought in, theirs was a world that was far gentler, far less violent, very much more humane and innocent than mine.

I could not have expected them to understand an Indian's terror of symbols.

14

WITH THE COMING of winter the rains began and soon the lanes of Nashawy were knee-deep in cold, sticky mud and nobody ventured out of their houses if they could help it. Those were quiet days, for there was not much to do in the fields, apart from watering the winter wheat and taking the livestock out to pasture so that they could feed on freshly-cut maize and berseem. Cows and buffaloes would bear rich loads of milk during these months, if fed properly, so every family that could afford to had planted fodder crops, and those that hadn't were buying fresh feed from others. No house wanted to be without its supply of milk now, for in this season everyone relished the thought of sitting at home, away from the cold, and talking and resting through the day and eating plentifully of yoghurt, cheese and ghee.

One morning, eager for a break from the long days I had spent sitting in smoke-filled rooms, I took advantage of a sudden clearing of the skies and set out for the fields with a book. It took a while to get through the muddy lanes, but once the village was behind me it seemed well worth it. The countryside was extraordinarily beautiful at this time of year: whenever there was a clear day the wheat, clover and maize stood brilliantly green against deep blue skies, while Nashawy itself, with its huddle of earth houses, seemed like a low range of hills brooding in the distance.

I took a path that led past Khamees's land, for I often stopped by to talk to him or his brothers when I went out for a walk. They were usually to be found sitting in the spot where I had first met them, a shady knoll beside a canal, where two water-wheels stood side-by-side. One belonged to Khamees's family and the other to Zaghloul's, and they took it in turns to irrigate their fields at the times when water was released into the canal. They had planted trees there so that their cattle would have some shade while they were drawing the wheels, and since that was where they usually fed their livestock, they had also built a wooden water-trough, at one end of the clearing. It was a quiet, evocative spot, for there was a tranquil, sculptural quality to the great wooden disks of the water-wheels, lying half-buried in the leafy shade, with the tall maize standing like a green curtain against the background: in all of Nashawy there was no better place to read, especially when the wheels were turning and the water was gurgling slowly through the canals and into the fields. Neither Khamees nor his brothers were anywhere in sight when I arrived there, but I knew that one of them had to be close by for their family's livestock was tethered beside the trough—a buffalo, a cow, and a nanny-goat with great, pendulous udders. They were chewing contentedly on freshly-cut fodder, a great pile of a kind of maize called diréwa, grown specially for feeding livestock. I knew that it would not be long before Khamees or one of his brothers appeared and, eager to make the best of the silence, I settled down quickly to read.

I had only turned a page or two when there was a sudden rustling nearby, followed by a burst of giggles, and then Khamees's youngest brother, 'Eid, shot out of the maize field, carrying a sheaf of plants. He took shelter behind the trough, grinning delightedly, and moments later two girls burst into the clearing, hot on his heels. They came to an abrupt halt upon seeing me, and after looking me over, murmured their greetings. I had seen them before and knew them to be the daughters of men who had fields nearby; they were dressed in flowered skirts and headscarves, and they must have been about sixteen or so. They could not have been more than a couple of years older than 'Eid, but the difference seemed much greater, because 'Eid was unusually small for his age—a telescopically foreshortened version of Khamees.

At first my presence seemed to make the girls unsure of themselves, but my role as a harmless fixture was well established now, and they soon forgot about me and began to chase 'Eid round and round the water-wheel until finally his jallabeyya snagged on a beam and threw him to the ground.

The girls fell upon him where he lay, tickling and teasing, tugging his ears and pinching his knees. 'What's the matter, ya

'Eid, have you forgotten what you said?' one of them said, laughing. The other scratched him on the back and began to cajole, plaintively: 'Come on, ya 'Eid, you promised, you said you'd do it, now we're not leaving until you do.'

'Eid, gasping for breath, was in no state to answer until he finally managed to free himself and climb back on to his feet.

'No,' he said, with a masterful shake of his head while the two girls stood towering over him. 'No—can't you see I'm busy?'

At this, one of the girls pinned his arms back while the other began to tickle him and just when it seemed as though he would fall over yet again, he cried out loudly in surrender: 'Stop, stop that, you girls—wait a minute.'

The girls released him, but stood where they were, watchful and ready to spring. 'You said you'd help,' one of them said. 'Now you've got to do it.'

'All right,' he said, shrugging, haughtily. 'All right, all right, all right.'

He straightened his jallabeyya with a flourish and walked away from them, strutting like a prizefighter. As soon as his back was turned the girls ran past the livestock, exploding into giggles, and after pausing for a moment they raced into the maize field, vanishing as suddenly and mysteriously as they had come.

After they had gone, 'Eid tossed his head with a show of disdain and seated himself beside me. 'Did you see how they were behaving?' he said, crossing his arms across his chest. 'Did you see? Do you see how they've filled out; how they move their bodies when they walk? I'll tell you: what those two want is to get married. That's what they want, you understand—especially the big one, the one in the green dress—she wants to get married, she really wants it.'

Picking up a maize-leaf he began to chew on the stem, gazing narrow-eyed into the distance. 'Actually it's me they want to marry,' he said, after a long pause. 'Especially the big one, the one in the green dress; she really wants me—it's obvious. But I've made up my mind; I won't have her; she's too big for me. Why, if she rolled on me, I'd be finished. There'd be nothing left.'

There was a rustling sound in the maize again, and he jumped quickly to his feet. 'There, you see,' he said, with an air of world-weariness. 'You see—they just can't leave me alone. They're back again.'

When the two girls ran back into the clearing, a moment later, he cupped his hands around his mouth and announced: 'I've told him; I've told him how much you want to marry me.'

The girls stood transfixed for a moment, and then, with loud hoots of laughter they began to chase him around the trough again, tickling and slapping him playfully.

'Of course we'll marry you, ya 'Eid…'

'We'll both marry you…'

'As soon as you grow a little…'

'When you're a man…'

In a matter of seconds he was squealing and shouting, crying out to them to stop, but the chase went on until he had been reduced again to a squirming heap in the dust. Then, leaving him lying where he was, the girls vanished once again, suddenly and mysteriously.

'It's sad,' said 'Eid, once he had picked himself up again. 'It's sad how desperately they want to marry me. I want to get married too—it's about time now—but I don't want to marry them. They're no good; they're not pretty enough for me.'

'Who do you want to marry then?' I asked.

'I know the girl I would like to marry,' he said. 'She walks past here sometimes, on her way to her father's fields. I've said a few words to her, and from the way she smiles I know she would agree. But her parents wouldn't let her, so it's no use thinking of it.'

'Why not?' I said.

'Because she's in school, studying,' he said. 'And her people are well-off, while in our family we don't have very much and often things are very hard in our house. And apart from that, her father is a Badawy, and he probably wouldn't let her marry into our family. There's nothing I can do—in the end I'll probably have to marry one of my cousins, like my parents want.'

Then, squatting beside me, he explained that he hadn't told anyone in his family about the girl he wanted to marry: it was no use hoping that anything would come of it, because there had been trouble between the Jammal and the Badawy for a long time, since long before he was born. It went back to the days of a Badawy 'omda, one Ahmed Effendi, who had owned a lot of land around the village.

'Look over there,' said 'Eid, pointing with a stick. 'Do you see the land in front of us, from there to there, almost four feddans? That was all his land, and it still belongs to his son, who lives in Cairo. Khamees and I and my brothers, we work on it as sharecroppers—it doesn't belong to us. We only get a small part of the crop, he takes all the rest. We have some land of our own, which we got during the Reforms, but that's far away and it's not half as big as this.'

Ahmed Effendi, the old 'omda, had always treated the Jammal as though they were his slaves, said 'Eid. He had made them work without payment, in his house and on the fields, and as a result, once elections were started, the Jammal voted against him. There had been fights between the two clans afterwards and for a while it was just like a feud. Ahmed Effendi would gladly have evicted his Jammal tenants, but by then the law had changed and there was nothing he could do.

Towards the end of his story, Zaghloul the weaver appeared, leading a cow and a buffalo. He listened to 'Eid while giving his livestock their feed and then he seated himself beside us. Soon, in keeping with his habit, he piled a heap of freshly-shorn wool in front of him and began to spin yarn with a hand-held spindle.

When 'Eid had finished, Zaghloul broke in to say that he remembered Ahmed Effendi well; like every other man in the village he had often had to work on his fields. At the time of the harvest Ahmed Effendi had gone around the village, from door to door, with his watchmen in tow, and he'd left a sickle on the doorpost of every house which had an able-bodied man in it. Those who didn't turn out on his fields next morning ran the risk of being being beaten by his watchmen, with whips. Ahmed Effendi had been able to get away with anything he liked because he had had friends amongst the Pashas, powerful people who had connections with the British.

'And is it true, ya Zaghloul,' asked 'Eid, agog with curiosity, 'that whenever he saw a good-looking girl he would ask for her to be sent to him?'

'Yes,' said Zaghloul. 'When his eyes fell on a girl he would say to her relatives, "I want that woman in my house for the night," and sure enough, she would go, for there was nothing anyone could do. He had only to raise his voice and you would see twenty men throwing themselves in front of him, crying "at your service Effendi".'

'And what about you, ya Zaghloul?' said 'Eid, with a grin. 'Didn't you throw yourself flat in front of him so he could use you as he liked?'

Zaghloul smiled at him good-naturedly, his eyes vanishing into the folds of his prematurely wizened face. Then he turned to look at me, twirling his spindle in his hands.

'So what has our boy 'Eid been talking about?' he said. 'Has he been talking about the girl he's staring at nowadays?'

'Eid's eyes widened in shock. 'How did you know, ya Zaghloul?' he cried in astonishment. 'How did you know about that?'

'I know about these things,' said Zaghloul.

'But how could you know? Who was it who told you?'

'I've seen the way you stare at her,' said Zaghloul. 'No one had to tell me; it's clear enough, especially since you're at that age. If you're not careful, you'll find yourself saying "I'm in love," like a student or a college-boy. Watch what you're doing and don't forget you're a fellah: "love" is not for people like us.'

'Eid didn't answer; at the mention of the word 'love' he flushed red and darted off to replenish the stock of fodder that lay in front of his livestock. Busying himself with armloads of maize plants, he pretended not to hear what Zaghloul had said.

'What do you mean?' I asked Zaghloul. 'Why can't a fellah fall in love?'

'For us it only leads to trouble,' said Zaghloul. 'Love is for students and mowazzafeen and city people; they think about it all the time, just like they think of football. For us it's different; it's better not to think of it.'

'Eid was back now, his eyes wide with curiosity. 'How do you know, ya Zaghloul?' he said. 'Did it ever happen to you?'

'Something happened to me once,' Zaghloul said quietly,

fixing his gaze upon his twirling spindle. 'It began when I was a boy, about your age, fourteen or fifteen, and it went on for five whole years. She was a girl from the city, the daughter of a relative of ours who had a job in Alexandria. Her father would come down with all of them once every summer to visit his family in Nashawy. I had known her all my life, but that summer when we were fourteen, I saw her when she came to the village, and suddenly everything changed. We would talk sometimes, for we were relatives after all, and I would try to tell her things, but I could never find the words. You know, she and her family used to sleep in a house that was in the centre of the village, a long way from where we lived. But when she was in Nashawy, I was never able to sleep. I would steal out late at night and go silently across the village, and when I reached their house, I would put my ear to the crack in her door and listen to her breathing in her sleep; it was like my life was in her breath. And that was how I lived for five years, waiting for her to come to the village for a few days in the summer so that I could listen to the sound of her breath at night, kneeling by her door. And all the while my family kept trying to get me married, and every time I'd say no, no, not yet, and in my heart I would think of her and the day when she would come back again to Nashawy.'

'Eid cocked his head to look into Zaghloul's lowered face. 'So what happened, ya Zaghloul?' he said. 'Why didn't you try to marry her?'

'My father wouldn't hear of it,' said Zaghloul. 'I told him once, to his face I told him—I want to marry that girl and none other. But he said to me: "Get that idea out of your head; you'll never marry her. We want a girl for you who can work in the fields and milk the cattle and sweep away the cow dung. She's a city girl, that one, she doesn't know how we live." I wanted to tell him that I loved her, but I knew he would slap me if I did, so I kept my peace, and later that year he arranged for me to marry a girl from the village, one of his cousin's daughters, and that was that, khalas.'

There was a tight, lopsided little smile on his shrunken face as he looked up and nodded at 'Eid.

'But I was lucky,' he said. 'At least I didn't lose my reason like some men do. If you go through Nashawy and the next village and the village after that and you ask everyone how many mad people there are and what it was that drove them mad, you'll see that there was one reason and one alone: it was love. That's what happens, ya 'Eid, that's why you have to be careful and mind what you're doing.'

'Eid rubbed his chin, frowning reflectively. 'But in the city,' he said, 'they all fall in love—in Cairo and Alexandria and Damanhour. You can see it on TV.'

'Things are different there,' said Zaghloul. 'All kinds of things happen in cities: why, do you know they have places there where women will let their bodies be used, for just a few pounds?'

He nodded sagely as 'Eid stared at him, in speechless astonishment. 'Yes,' he said, warming to his theme, 'that's right, there are houses in Alexandria where men pay five hundred pounds to spend a night with a woman—five hundred pounds, for one night!'

He paused to reflect, chewing on his lip, remembering perhaps that the sum he had just quoted was equal to the figure his harvest of cotton earned him in a year. 'Of course,' he added quickly, 'that includes food and other things—turkey, whiskey and things like that.'

'Eid, goggle-eyed in wonder, cried: 'And do they all cost that much—five hundred pounds?'

'No,' said Zaghloul, 'not all—some are as cheap as five pounds and some take just a pound and a half. But that's just for a couple of hours, or even less.'

'Where, ya Zaghloul?' said 'Eid, prodding him eagerly with his elbow. 'Where can one find these houses? Tell me.'

Zaghloul shook his head vaguely. 'My cousin worked in Alexandria,' he said, 'for a few months in the winter, and the men he worked with used to go to those places. He told me about them, but he never went himself—one can't really.'

'But where are those places, ya Zaghloul?' cried 'Eid. 'Tell me—on which street? I'd like to go and see one of those places.'

Zaghloul smiled at him gently. 'They'd make a fool of you, ya 'Eid,' he said. 'They'd feel your face, like this, and ask for five pounds. They'd stroke your chest, like this, and ask for ten. They'd reach under your jallabeyya, like this, and ask for fifty, and before they were done, you'd lose everything your father possesses.'

'We'll see about that,' said 'Eid, 'just tell me where those places are.'

They began to laugh, but soon their laughter died away, and they fell silent, squatting on their heels—tiny 'Eid, too small for his age, and bandy-legged, prematurely wizened Zaghloul—they smiled and rubbed their groins and scratched their thighs as they sat there, day-dreaming about forbidden pleasures in faraway cities.

Presently 'Eid said: 'Why do they do it, those girls? Do their families make them?'

'Yes,' said Zaghloul. 'That's what happens; their families put them up to it. They take thirty pounds a month from the owner of the house and that's that, khalas—they leave their daughters there and the owners are free to do what they like with them.'

'Eid grinned and shot him a glance. 'And how much do you charge for your wife, ya Zaghloul?' he said. 'Fifteen pounds? I'll pay it, will you let me?'

'It'll cost more than you can afford,' Zaghloul said, smiling at him, unmoved.

Then, turning to me, he added: 'Don't take offence: we fellaheen, we love to joke; "our blood is light," as people say.'

'Oh the black day!' cried 'Eid, jumping to his feet, as though he could not contain himself any longer. 'I'd really like to go to one of those places.'

He ran across to the trough, where the livestock were feeding, and put his arm around his nanny-goat. 'Look how I love her,' he shouted, planting a kiss on her face.

Later, on the way back to Nashawy, I came across Khamees, riding out to the fields on his donkey. He climbed off when he saw me, and after we had exchanged greetings and talked for a while, he asked casually: 'Did you see 'Eid on your way? Was he feeding the livestock, out by the water-wheel?'

'Yes,' I said, 'that's just where I'm coming from.'

'Was there anyone else there?' he asked, watching me closely.

'There was Zaghloul,' I said. 'We were all sitting there talking.'

'No one else?'

'A couple of girls dropped by,' I said, 'just for a minute or two.'

Khamees struck his forehead with a loud, despairing cry: 'Oh the Protector, oh the Lord! That dog 'Eid is going to bring my family to ruin. What were those girls doing? Go on, tell me.'

'Nothing,' I stammered, taken aback; it seemed wholly out of character for Khamees to be overcome by moral indignation. 'Nothing at all, they just came by for a minute…'

'Tell me something,' he said, shaking my arm. 'Tell me, try to remember—were they, by any chance, carrying away our fodder?'

It dawned on me that Khamees was right: the girls had carried away armloads of fodder every time they ran out of the clearing. The reason for their cultivation of 'Eid's friendship was suddenly clear to me.

Khamees read the answer on my face, and at once, hitching up his jallabeyya, he jumped on his donkey.

'That 'Eid is going to ruin our whole family,' he cried. 'Those girls tickle him and tease him and he ends up giving away all our fodder—the fool, he thinks they like him.'

He struck his donkey on the rump, and as it trotted away he turned around in his seat to call out to me. 'What that boy needs is a wife,' he shouted; 'we'll get him married to one of our cousins—that'll help him understand life and its difficulties.'

15

'A COUPLE OF years after you left Egypt,' said Shaikh Musa, 'I heard some news about your friend Khamees and his family, and I thought—this is something the doktór would like to know.'

He paused to prod the embers of his shusha, and settled back in his divan.

A friend of his, he said, had stopped by in Lataifa one day, on